MW00712078

WHEN THE COPS COME KNOCKIN'

An Illustrated Guide to Criminal Law

School and Organization Edition

Written by Travis Townsend and Trinity Townsend

*A book designed to teach young people (and anyone else) about criminal law,
the criminal justice system, and legal rights*

TORINITY

DISCLAIMER

Warning: the explanations provided throughout *When the Cops Come Knockin'* are not intended to be precise recitations of the law, but instead are loose, worst-case–scenario translations of the law aimed at giving the reader a surface understanding of the law. The definitions of specified laws in this book are loosely based on the model penal code and common law and may not be in effect in the jurisdiction and city where you live. By writing this book, we are not providing legal advice and do not attempt to provide legal advice. Readers assume the risk of acting upon the information found in *When the Cops Come Knockin'*. We recommend you contact an attorney with respect to any and all of the subject matter inside this book for clarification, and if you find yourself in legal trouble, hire an attorney immediately or, if you can't afford one, ask to have the court appoint an attorney to you immediately!

All the trademarks or brands in this document are registered by their respective owner.

Table of Contents

Acknowledgements

Numerous people were helpful, supportive, and inspirational in the production and development of this book. We would be absolutely remiss if we did not thank them for all of their honesty, guidance, and encouragement. We give our thanks to:

Joann Odneal, Travis Townsend, Sr., Keith Townsend, and all of our extended Townsend and Curry family; Charlene Brown, Delvon Parker, Stephanie Meister, Jon Royce, Sheri McCurdy-Knox, Eric Simon, Lashay Callaway, Willie Raby, Michael Griffin, Paul Castenada, Justice Barber, Brandon Williams, Cassandra Tucker, Robert Reid, Natasha Bell, Andre Hewitt, Martha Duncan, Dwyone Joiner, Tamera Woodard, Shauna Hill, Julia Trankiem, Selia Acevedo, Deidre Frances, Yale Kamisar, Robert Daniel, Brooke Reynolds, Christopher Reynolds, Ciji Tatum, Kenneth Turk, Felicia LeRay, Diego Bernal, James Forman, Jr., Bernard Coleman, and Konteint Redmon

Any and all errors and omissions are, of course, entirely attributable to the authors.

Introduction

"Ignorance of the law excuses no man; not that all men know the law, but because it is an excuse every man will plead, and no man can tell how to confute him."

— John Selden

"Who will protect the public when the police violate the law?"

— William Ramsey Clark

Though all of us are subject to them, very few of us actually understand the justice system and criminal law. This is fine until we find ourselves or our loved ones ensnared in them. In certain communities, crimes and their justice system punishments are as much a part of life as air and water. This is especially true of urban areas and areas of high poverty.

Schools in these areas focus on the typical vital subjects of reading, writing, math, science, and social studies, and these subjects are certainly necessary so that each student will have the knowledge and skills to navigate, survive, and thrive in society.

It is our opinion, as the writers of this book, however, that schools—especially those whose student populations come from high-crime, high-poverty communities—fail to teach their students an equally vital subject—criminal law. After all, what good is

mastering all of the standard school subjects if you are incarcerated and cannot use the skills learned?

Criminal law is really "the missing subject." In our opinion it may be just as important as any of the other subjects taught in middle and high school. We believe that all middle and high schools, juvenile court systems, and at-risk youth programs should have an instructional framework that educates children and young adults (and even older adults) about crime, criminal laws, and the inevitable consequences that result from breaking the law.

The basic premise of this book is that an ounce of prevention is worth a pound of the cure. Just as getting a vaccination protects against acquiring a horrible disease in the future, knowing the law and how to protect and assert your rights can prevent tragic legal consequences. These consequences can range from having to pay astronomically high attorney fees and going through the emotional distress of hearings and trials to ultimately being incarcerated or watching a loved one being put behind bars for a long time.

When the Cops Come Knockin' is a worst-case interpretation of complex criminal law and procedure concepts and rules. These concepts and rules are put into plain English for all to understand. The content of this book includes simple explanations of your rights and descriptions of criminal laws for which you can be punished for violating.

When the Cops Come Knockin' also discusses defenses to criminal charges, provides guidance on how to behave when encountering the police, and suggests strategies for staying out of trouble with the law. Through explanations and illustrations, this book uses real-world examples to help readers understand difficult criminal law and procedure concepts.

It is the sincerest desire of the authors that after reading *When the Cops Come Knockin'* readers will come away with knowledge that will help them to make positive choices.

Why This Book?

A key goal of this book is to help the reader develop an understanding of the law. This book will provide the reader with opportunities to think about how the criminal laws, the criminal justice system, and the reader's behavior impact his or her life.

This book will also help the reader think about past, current, and future actions and will impart knowledge that will, we hope, help the reader avoid or cope with potential situations involving the criminal justice system. Readers are encouraged to make notes, highlight, and write in this book. Feel free to record questions, things discovered, feelings, thoughts, lessons learned, important words, and reflections. There are recaps and reflective questions throughout the book that will aid in remembering and applying learned terms and concepts.

Pre-Assessment

Directions

Before you begin reading this book, please take a few moments to answer the following questions to see how much you already know about information that will be covered throughout. Please check the number of the answer that represents your awareness of criminal law, the legal system, and/or how to protect your rights.

GENERAL AWARENESS OF THE LAW

ANSWER	RATING
Strongly Agree	5
Agree	4
Uncertain	3
Disagree	2
Strongly Disagree	1

1. I have a clear understanding of criminal law, the legal system, and how to protect my legal rights.

    ☐ 5 ☐ 4 ☐ 3 ☐ 2 ☐ 1

2. I have a clear understanding of what a crime is.

    ☐ 5 ☐ 4 ☐ 3 ☐ 2 ☐ 1

3. I have a clear understanding of what makes a person a criminal.

    ☐ 5 ☐ 4 ☐ 3 ☐ 2 ☐ 1

4. I have a clear understanding of what laws are.

    ☐ 5 ☐ 4 ☐ 3 ☐ 2 ☐ 1

5. I have a clear understanding of why laws are important.

    ☐ 5 ☐ 4 ☐ 3 ☐ 2 ☐ 1

6. I can explain the concept of willful blindness.

    ☐ 5 ☐ 4 ☐ 3 ☐ 2 ☐ 1

7. I have a clear understanding of what criminal negligence is.

    ☐ 5 ☐ 4 ☐ 3 ☐ 2 ☐ 1

8. I have a clear understanding of what criminal recklessness is.

    ☐ 5 ☐ 4 ☐ 3 ☐ 2 ☐ 1

9. I can explain how not thinking and caring about my actions can lead to my being punished for a crime.

☐ 5 ☐ 4 ☐ 3 ☐ 2 ☐ 1

10. I can define the crime of larceny.

☐ 5 ☐ 4 ☐ 3 ☐ 2 ☐ 1

11. I can recognize the difference between the crimes of burglary and robbery.

☐ 5 ☐ 4 ☐ 3 ☐ 2 ☐ 1

12. I know what bullying is and its consequences.

☐ 5 ☐ 4 ☐ 3 ☐ 2 ☐ 1

13. I know how to fight against bullying.

☐ 5 ☐ 4 ☐ 3 ☐ 2 ☐ 1

14. I can describe different situations in which a person could be charged with murder.

☐ 5 ☐ 4 ☐ 3 ☐ 2 ☐ 1

15. I can distinguish between murder and involuntary manslaughter.

☐ 5 ☐ 4 ☐ 3 ☐ 2 ☐ 1

16. I understand what an inchoate crime is and can name several.

☐ 5 ☐ 4 ☐ 3 ☐ 2 ☐ 1

17. I can define the crime of conspiracy.

☐ 5 ☐ 4 ☐ 3 ☐ 2 ☐ 1

18. I can describe what an accomplice to a crime is.

☐ 5 ☐ 4 ☐ 3 ☐ 2 ☐ 1

19. I understand what a strict liability crime is.

☐ 5 ☐ 4 ☐ 3 ☐ 2 ☐ 1

20. I can explain the difference between statutory rape and rape.

☐ 5 ☐ 4 ☐ 3 ☐ 2 ☐ 1

21. I can recognize situations and circumstances that might lead to my involvement in criminal behavior.

☐ 5 ☐ 4 ☐ 3 ☐ 2 ☐ 1

22. I have a good understanding of my rights regarding searches and seizures.

☐ 5 ☐ 4 ☐ 3 ☐ 2 ☐ 1

23. I understand the dangers of "sexting" and cyberbullying.

☐ 5 ☐ 4 ☐ 3 ☐ 2 ☐ 1

24. I understand the dangers of playing with fire.

☐ 5 ☐ 4 ☐ 3 ☐ 2 ☐ 1

25. I understand the consequences of underage drinking.

☐ 5   ☐ 4   ☐ 3   ☐ 2   ☐ 1

26. I understand what disorderly conduct and obstruction of justice are.

☐ 5   ☐ 4   ☐ 3   ☐ 2   ☐ 1

27. I understand what legal defenses are and can name a few.

☐ 5   ☐ 4   ☐ 3   ☐ 2   ☐ 1

28. I have a clear understanding of what constitutes self-defense and what does not.

☐ 5   ☐ 4   ☐ 3   ☐ 2   ☐ 1

29. I know what unlawful force is.

☐ 5   ☐ 4   ☐ 3   ☐ 2   ☐ 1

30. I understand the rules for defending my property.

☐ 5   ☐ 4   ☐ 3   ☐ 2   ☐ 1

31. I understand when the law requires a duty to help a person in danger.

☐ 5   ☐ 4   ☐ 3   ☐ 2   ☐ 1

32. I understand what to do if I have contact with the police.

☐ 5   ☐ 4   ☐ 3   ☐ 2   ☐ 1

33. I have a clear understanding of what probable cause is.

☐ 5   ☐ 4   ☐ 3   ☐ 2   ☐ 1

34. I can articulate the difference between probable cause and reasonable suspicion.

☐ 5   ☐ 4   ☐ 3   ☐ 2   ☐ 1

35. I can explain what a search warrant is and what to look for when reading one.

☐ 5   ☐ 4   ☐ 3   ☐ 2   ☐ 1

36. I understand the difference between a search warrant and an arrest warrant.

☐ 5   ☐ 4   ☐ 3   ☐ 2   ☐ 1

37. I have a clear understanding of what an arrest is.

☐ 5   ☐ 4   ☐ 3   ☐ 2   ☐ 1

38. I can explain the importance of the Constitution of the United States as it applies to my rights when dealing with law enforcement.

☐ 5   ☐ 4   ☐ 3   ☐ 2   ☐ 1

39. I understand the concept of "expectation of privacy" as it applies to citizens' rights when dealing with law enforcement.

☐ 5   ☐ 4   ☐ 3   ☐ 2   ☐ 1

40. I have a clear understanding of how to speak to the police.

   ☐ 5 ☐ 4 ☐ 3 ☐ 2 ☐ 1

41. I know what to do if the police want to enter my home, but do not have a search warrant.

   ☐ 5 ☐ 4 ☐ 3 ☐ 2 ☐ 1

42. I know which Constitutional Amendments give me my rights against the police unreasonably searching and seizing my things or myself.

   ☐ 5 ☐ 4 ☐ 3 ☐ 2 ☐ 1

43. I have a clear understanding of what things to do to prevent the police from raiding any party that I throw.

   ☐ 5 ☐ 4 ☐ 3 ☐ 2 ☐ 1

44. I have a clear understanding of what to do if the police want to arrest me at my house.

   ☐ 5 ☐ 4 ☐ 3 ☐ 2 ☐ 1

45. I understand when and how to ask for an attorney if I am arrested.

   ☐ 5 ☐ 4 ☐ 3 ☐ 2 ☐ 1

46. I have a clear understanding of what behaviors and clothing styles bring on police attention.

   ☐ 5 ☐ 4 ☐ 3 ☐ 2 ☐ 1

47. I understand how to handle a situation in which the police want to search my car.

   ☐ 5 ☐ 4 ☐ 3 ☐ 2 ☐ 1

48. I understand what to do if I get pulled over by the police.

   ☐ 5 ☐ 4 ☐ 3 ☐ 2 ☐ 1

49. I can recognize when the police are supposed to read me my rights.

   ☐ 5 ☐ 4 ☐ 3 ☐ 2 ☐ 1

50. I know what rights I have if I am arrested.

   ☐ 5 ☐ 4 ☐ 3 ☐ 2 ☐ 1

PART I
CRIMES AND CRIMINAL OFFENSES

Chapter 1
Crime and Punishment

IMPORTANT WORDS
Crime
Criminal
Laws
Punishment

What Is a Criminal?

To begin to understand the ins and outs of criminal law, first you have to know what a crime is and what makes a person a criminal. Basically, a *crime* is breaking a government rule that the government punishes people for breaking. For instance, there are government rules that forbid people from breaking into people's houses and taking their stuff. If you break into a person's house and steal his or her stuff, you are breaking a government rule. In other words, you committed a crime. If you get caught, you'll be punished. And of course, because you committed a crime, you would now be classified as a *criminal*.

Another definition of the word criminal is this: a person who the government punishes for causing a certain result that the government doesn't like to see. For example, the government doesn't like to see people losing their lives from gun violence for no good reason. So, the government has a rule stating that people can't shoot guns at other people without a legally justifiable reason. If you were to shoot and kill somebody in cold blood, you would have caused a result that the government didn't want to see—the death of a person from gun violence for no legally justifiable reason. So while shooting a gun is not always a crime, you would be a criminal because, by shooting the gun, you caused a result the government does not want to see.

Do you have to be a "bad" person to be branded a criminal? Definitely not. Good people sometimes break government rules. They'll still be considered criminals. For example, a desperate mother with no money might steal food to feed her hungry children. Would you consider her a "bad" person? Probably not. But, in the eyes of the law, she's a criminal. The point is that you don't have to be a bad person or intend to cause bad things to happen to be branded a criminal.

Laws

Government rules are better known as *laws*. Laws cover a lot of punishable stuff—from murder and armed robbery to cursing in front of women and children (yes, in some communities you can actually be punished for cursing).

Laws are created mostly to keep order and to protect people. If there were no laws, nobody would be safe. From requiring people to buckle up when driving to making it a crime for people to break into your car, laws help make life safer for everybody.

Most people would probably agree that we need laws to keep people from doing wrong and to make sure they do right. Sometimes, though, it might seem as if some laws were created just to hassle people. No matter what you think about criminal laws, if you don't follow them, you're a criminal.

Punishment

Laws are only useful when we all agree to follow them. And when you don't follow the laws, count on being hit with consequences—very unpleasant consequences. The government has a lot of punishments it can hit you with for breaking the law. These punishments could be anything from making you pay money (fines), to taking away certain privileges (such as suspending your driver's license), to locking you up in prison. The threat of punishment is supposed to discourage you from committing crimes.

To Sum Up

It's important to obey the laws. It doesn't matter if you're a good person at heart—if you break the law, you will be punished.

CHAPTER RECAP
Concept Review of Chapter 1

- A crime can be defined as the breaking of a government rule that the government punishes people for breaking.

- Breaking a government rule is what makes a person a criminal.

- Causing a result that the government does not like to see is also what makes a person a criminal.

- You do not have to be a "bad" or "evil" person to be a criminal.

- Laws are rules created by the government to maintain order.

- Failure to follow the laws results in punishment from the government.

THINK ABOUT IT
Reflection #1

Have you or someone you know ever been a victim of a crime? If so, what happened? Has crime affected you or someone you know in a way other than being a victim?

Chapter 2
Thinking and Caring

Most of the time, people who get punished for breaking the law are fully aware that they were doing something unlawful. We say that the person's acts were *intentional*. For instance, let's say that Jon-Jon wants Malcolm's 28-inch rims and decides to steal them. After waiting until 3:00 a.m., he goes to Malcolm's apartment complex, and while Malcolm is asleep, he steals the rims off his truck, leaving it on blocks.

The above example is a clear case of a guy intentionally causing a criminal result. Jon-Jon knew that he was doing something illegal. But did you know that the government can say that you intentionally broke the law even if you didn't know you were doing something illegal? Believe it or not, if you *should have known* you were breaking the law, the government can still accuse you of intentionally breaking the law!

When it comes to breaking the law, ignorance is no excuse. In fact, if something you are about to do seems as though it might be illegal, you shouldn't ignore the warning signs and go through with it. If you get caught, you'll be treated as if you absolutely knew you were breaking the law. Ignoring

clues that should let you know that you are doing, or are about to do, something illegal is called *willful blindness*.

Here is an example of how being willfully blind can lead to being charged for intentionally breaking the law:

Your cousin, who was just released from prison a few months ago for dealing drugs, asks you to drop off a package at a certain address on your way home. You are a little suspicious that drugs could be involved because your cousin is a convicted drug dealer. But he's your cousin, and you figure if you don't ask him any details about what's in the package, you won't be purposely doing anything wrong if it turns out drugs are involved. So you say yes. You head out with the package in hand. As you're approaching the door of the house where you're supposed to drop the package off, the cops pull up in their cruiser. They tell you, "Stay right there!" They get out of the car with a drug-sniffing dog and he goes crazy barking at the package under your arm. Turns out there are drugs in the package. The cops tell you you're under arrest, handcuff you, and read you your rights. They charge you with drug trafficking.

Now, where did you go wrong in this situation? You went wrong when you decided to ignore what seemed like a possible drug delivery. The police won't care that your cousin never told you what was in the package and they won't care that you never opened it. You knew the situation seemed suspicious and you purposely ignored the warning signs. As far as the law is concerned, your act of dealing drugs was intentional. Remember, if you ignored facts that could have made you aware you were breaking the law, you will be accused of willful blindness. Basically, in the eyes of the law, your acts are intentional whenever you knew or should have known that you were doing something illegal. So you should always be aware of, and avoid, suspicious situations.

Risky Business

Taking risks is an important and necessary part of life. But when those risks lead to the possible injury or death of others, you should think twice. The law punishes people who, because of risky behavior, end up hurting or killing other people—even if they didn't mean to hurt or kill anybody. Two important things that you should come away with from reading this book are that you should always THINK and CARE about the consequences of your actions.

Let's take a look at an example of how not thinking about the consequences of her actions could cause a person to be charged with a serious crime:

Tamika leaves her four-year-old daughter home alone after putting her to bed. She goes out to the club because she doesn't expect her daughter to wake up until well after she's returned home. Unfortunately, her daughter wakes up before Tamika makes it back. She calls for Tamika, but receives no answer. She's hungry and decides to cook some hot dogs on the stove; after all, she's seen Tamika do it plenty of times. She turns one of the burners on and puts the hot dogs in a pot of water. After the hot dogs have been boiling for a while, the child tries to grab the pot but ends up overturning it, scalding herself in the process. She runs out the front door screaming for her mother. Hearing the screaming child, a neighbor calls the police.

When the cops catch up to Tamika, she will probably be charged with child endangerment because she was *criminally negligent*. Criminal negligence is when you do something that you should have known could end up getting somebody hurt. It doesn't matter if it never came to your mind that somebody could get hurt—if they're hurt, it's thanks to you.

In the above example, Tamika didn't think that her daughter could get hurt if she left her home alone. But there are reasons why people shouldn't leave a young child home alone. Any number of tragic things could happen—and most folks know this. Tamika should have known, too. Besides possible jail time, Tamika's failure to think about the consequences of her risky actions might result in her daughter being taken away from her.

Even worse than not thinking about the consequences of your actions is not caring about the consequences. In the eyes of the law, not caring that your actions could lead to somebody getting hurt is especially serious. If you do something risky that you *know* could lead to somebody getting hurt, you could be accused of being *criminally reckless*.

Most people know that tossing rocks off an overpass onto the windshields of oncoming cars can lead to somebody being hurt or killed. But some people do it anyway because they really don't care what might happen. The reality is that if somebody is injured or killed because of a tossed rock landing on a windshield, the person tossing

the rocks is going to be looking at some serious punishment. This is because he is being criminally reckless. He may have no intention of actually hurting or killing anybody, but the fact that he just doesn't care if somebody does get hurt or killed is enough to accuse him of intentionally hurting somebody.

Some people play with guns, some drive drunk, and some make pipe bombs. It's important to care about what might happen from doing these risky things. Even if you don't care that you might hurt or kill yourself or somebody else, the fact that you could spend a large part of your life in prison should give you serious pause.

To Sum Up

Using your brain is probably the best way to avoid getting into trouble with the law. You need to use your brain to be aware of what's going on around you and to THINK and CARE about the possible consequences of your actions.

CHAPTER RECAP

Concept Review of Chapter 2

- A crime is considered intentional if you commit it knowing that you were doing something unlawful or if you should have known that you were doing something unlawful.

- Ignoring or pretending not to recognize things that would let you know that you are involved, or about to be involved, in illegal activity is called willful blindness.

- If you should have known that you were doing something illegal, you will be punished as if you did know.

- Criminal negligence is when you, unthinkingly, do something you should have known could result in somebody getting hurt.

- If you do something risky that you know could lead to somebody getting hurt, but go through with it anyway—you can be accused of being criminally reckless.

THINK ABOUT IT
Reflection #2

Why is it important to THINK and CARE about the consequences of your actions? What types of activities do you currently engage in that you should probably think and care more about? Please explain why.

Chapter 3
Theft Crimes

IMPORTANT WORDS
Larceny
Embezzlement
Robbery
Burglary

Taking other people's property is one of the oldest criminal acts. In the past, you could have your hand cut off for stealing. Today, you'll be able to keep your hand—count on losing your freedom instead. Here, the focus will be on four types of theft crimes—larceny, embezzlement, robbery, and burglary.

Larceny

Larceny is taking somebody else's property with the intent to keep it. It is better known as stealing.

An interesting fact about larceny of store items (also known as shoplifting) is that you can be charged with larceny even if you don't walk out of the store with the goods. As soon as you pick up the items with the intent to steal them and walk a few inches from where you got them, the law says that you have carried the items away.

Now, you might wonder how the authorities would know that you intended to steal. Well, whenever you do something suspicious, such as stuff an item into your purse or pockets, it's assumed that you intended to steal the item. Let's say Andrea opens a T-shirt package and puts the T-shirt on right in the store. If the security people swoop down on her at that moment, she can be charged with larceny. But what if she was going to pay for the T-shirt once she got to the register? That doesn't matter. If Andrea didn't make it to the register before the security people got to her, she shouldn't be surprised if she gets hit with a larceny charge.

Did you know that you can be charged with a crime for accepting or buying stuff that you know is stolen? The police don't have to be able to read your mind to figure out if you actually knew the goods were stolen. They simply look at the situation and ask if you should have known you were accepting stolen stuff. For instance, let's say there's a guy who sells laptops from the trunk of his car at thirty percent off what they cost at the store. Plus, he only takes cash and doesn't give receipts. Because of all the "warning signs," you should know that the laptops are stolen. If you were to buy a laptop from this person, the cops will charge you as if you knew that the product was stolen—because you should have known that the product was stolen. (Remember the dangers of being willfully blind?)

Embezzlement

Embezzlement is when somebody puts you in charge of his or her stuff to manage, but you decide to make it yours without permission from the person who gave it to you. In other words, it's a theft crime.

The most common victims of embezzlement are employers. Hooking yourself up at the job can often be considered embezzlement. For instance, say you have a job at a corner store. Your boss trusts you to keep track of how much money the store makes and to deposit the money at the bank. Because she doesn't really know how much money the store takes in, you decide to fudge the numbers, keep a little of the money for yourself, and deposit the rest. That is embezzlement. The money you kept wasn't yours—it belonged to your boss. You were in charge of depositing all of the money, but instead, you stole some of it.

Embezzlement isn't just limited to the business world; it happens in the drug game, too. Say a drug boss gives his street dealers some drugs to sell. The dealers are supposed to hit the corners, sell the dope, and then give the money to the boss, who then gives them their cut. Sometimes, one of the street dealers will tell the boss that somebody robbed him of the money he made that day. He'll claim that he doesn't have any money to give to the boss. What the boss doesn't know, though, is that the corner dealer pocketed all of the money for himself. The low-level dealer has just embezzled from his boss. The only difference is that if the boss in this case finds out, the low-level dealer won't be looking at possibly going to prison. Instead, he'll probably receive the death penalty—street style.

Robbery

Robbery is when somebody takes another person's stuff (such as a chain or watch) right off the person or in front of the person by using force or threatening to use force. The robber may even threaten to hurt somebody who's with the person being robbed. Using a deadly weapon to carry out the robbery changes the robbery into the more serious charge of armed robbery.

Pages 15–17 show examples of robbery, some of which you might easily recognize and some that might surprise you.

Burglary

Burglary is when you illegally, or without proper permission, go into a building or home with the intent to commit a crime (such as stealing) once inside. You don't actually have to "break" into a building to commit burglary. In fact, you could enter the building through a wide-open door. So forget about having to do something dramatic such as blowing up the lock on the building with explosives or throwing a brick through the back window and then climbing through. It's entering without permission that makes it "breaking in."

The moment you go into a building or home without permission and with the intent to commit a crime, you could be on the hook for burglary. And how does the law know that you intended to commit a

A BULLY GOES UP TO A KID IN THE SCHOOL YARD AND TELLS HIM TO FORK OVER HIS LUNCH MONEY OR ELSE TAKE A POUNDIN'.

A THUG ROLLS UP ON A STORE CASHIER, PULLS OUT A GUN AND ORDERS HER TO EMPTY THE REGISTER.

crime while inside? They simply assume you intended to based purely on the fact that you broke in. This makes sense because most people don't break into buildings or houses unless they intend to commit a crime.

A quick note: If you enter a building that is open to the public during hours of operation with the intent to commit a crime, you won't be charged with burglary. Instead, you'll be charged with the crime you intended to commit once you got inside the building. For example, stealing electronics from a store that's open would get you a larceny charge, not a burglary charge. But breaking in and stealing electronics from a closed store would get you a burglary charge.

To Sum Up

Taking other people's things is something that the government does not tolerate. Whether you steal by trickery or force, you will be punished once caught.

CHAPTER RECAP
Concept Review of Chapter 3

- Larceny is another word for stealing or theft. It is the wrongful taking of somebody else's property with the intent to never give it back.

- You can be charged with a crime for accepting or buying stolen goods.

- The offense of shoplifting doesn't require that you leave a store with the goods. Actions that can be construed as showing your intent to steal (removing tags or putting merchandise in your pockets) can put you on the hook for shoplifting.

- Embezzlement occurs when somebody gives you his or her property to hold or take care of, but you decide to make it yours without permission from the person who gave it to you.

- Robbery occurs when somebody steals somebody else's property right off the person or in front of the person by using force or threatening to use force.

- Burglary occurs when a person illegally, or without proper permission, goes into a building or home with the intent to commit a crime once inside.

THINK ABOUT IT
Reflection #3

Why do you think people commit theft crimes? Can you think of ways to obtain things you want without committing theft crimes to get them? Please list some.

Chapter 4
Crimes Involving Violence

IMPORTANT WORDS
Battery
Aggravated Battery
Assault
Aggravated Assault
Homicide
Murder
Voluntary Manslaughter
Involuntary Manslaughter

Believe it or not, a simple schoolyard fight can get you put behind bars. What used to be "kids being kids" is often considered violent criminal behavior today. This is why you need to understand the crimes of battery and assault.

Battery

Battery can be defined as the unlawful use of force. So if you attack somebody without justification, you're committing battery. For instance, picking a fight with and hitting somebody is battery.

But battery isn't just limited to serious violence. Did you know that just touching somebody in an inappropriate way could be considered battery? In fact, pinching or grabbing somebody's body or body part(s) without his or her permission can be classified as battery. Even slapping books out of somebody's hand or knocking a hat off someone's head is battery. This is why it's usually a good idea to keep your hands to yourself.

Using weapons or objects to wrongfully touch somebody can lead to an *aggravated battery* charge. Aggravated battery is a serious form of battery that results in more severe punishment than what you would get for simple battery.

Assault

Now let's turn to the crime of assault. The interesting thing about assault is that you don't actually have to touch somebody physically to be charged with it. An *assault* can be one of two things. First, an assault can be an attempt to commit battery on somebody. An example would be if you were to swing a bat at somebody's head in an attempt to knock her out, but instead, you end up missing altogether. An assault can also be when you make somebody feel that you're going to physically hurt him at that moment. So, if you jump toward somebody with your shoulders raised, your fists balled up, and a scowl on your face as if you're going to punch him straight in the eye, you're actually committing an assault on that person.

Although assault and battery are two different crimes, they often go hand in hand. This is why people tend to get charged with "assault and battery." This makes sense if you think about it. Imagine that two guys,

BATTERY IS WHEN YOU TOUCH SOMEBODY IN A WAY THAT OFFENDS THEM OR WHEN THEY DON'T WANT YOU TO. AN EXAMPLE OF THIS IS WHEN YOU PUNCH SOMEBODY WITHOUT JUSTIFICATION.

ASSAULT IS WHEN YOU TRY TO COMMIT A BATTERY ON SOMEBODY. FOR INSTANCE, IF YOU TAKE A SWING AT A GUY WITHOUT JUSTIFICATION AND MISS, YOU'VE ASSAULTED THE GUY.

Arthur and Bill, are arguing with each other. If Arthur balls up his fist and jumps at Bill with a right hook that connects with Bill's face, Arthur is guilty of committing assault and battery on Bill. The assault was committed when Bill saw Arthur lunge at him with his fist coming toward his face. The battery was committed when Arthur's punch connected.

Using a weapon or dangerous object to assault a person is called *aggravated assault.* For example, if you were to grab a knife and rush somebody, the knife makes the crime aggravated assault. If you were to use only your fists, the crime would be simply assault. Just like with aggravated battery, aggravated assault carries stiffer punishments than simple assault.

Homicides

A *homicide* is defined as a killing of a human being by another person. There are a lot of different times and ways people kill other people. Sometimes a homicide is a crime and sometimes it isn't. The text below discusses the homicides that are crimes and how you may be charged with a crime for committing a homicide. The three homicide crimes that will be discussed are murder, voluntary manslaughter, and involuntary manslaughter.

Murder

The "biggie" of the homicide crimes, *murder* is considered the worst because it often involves plotting and planning to kill someone or acting with a total disregard for human life. Because of the severity of the crime, the government punishes murder more harshly than just about all other crimes. In some states, you can even be put to death for committing murder.

See the examples on pages 25–28 to learn how you can catch a murder charge.

Voluntary Manslaughter

When you intentionally kill somebody because you were seriously provoked and lost control before you had time to cool off, you have committed *voluntary manslaughter,* also known as a "heat of passion" killing. In other words, you were so shocked and got heated so quickly that you couldn't think straight and "lost it." Normally you'd get charged with murder, but because you were provoked, the crime gets knocked down to voluntary manslaughter. An example of voluntary manslaughter would be if a person you were arguing with suddenly backhanded you in the face. You instantly fill with rage, and right then and there, whip out your pocket knife and stab the guy, killing him in the process. Because your rage was instant and you acted before you could cool down, you might be charged with voluntary manslaughter instead of murder.

Keep in mind that you have to have been seriously provoked by something that would make a reasonable person "lose it" as you did. Words are not enough. If you kill somebody over something he or she said to you, you will be charged with murder. One last thing to keep in mind is that, if at any time you actually cooled down—even if for a moment—before killing the victim, you will be charged with murder.

Voluntary manslaughter is a very serious crime. While it often carries a slightly lighter penalty than murder, it usually entails serving serious time in prison. Keep this in mind

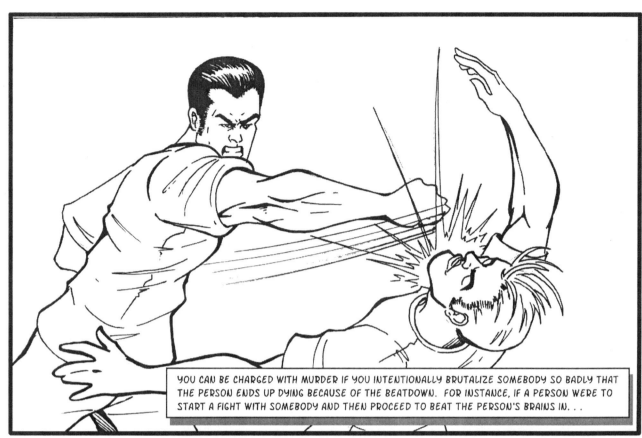

YOU CAN BE CHARGED WITH MURDER IF YOU INTENTIONALLY BRUTALIZE SOMEBODY SO BADLY THAT THE PERSON ENDS UP DYING BECAUSE OF THE BEATDOWN. FOR INSTANCE, IF A PERSON WERE TO START A FIGHT WITH SOMEBODY AND THEN PROCEED TO BEAT THE PERSON'S BRAINS IN. . .

HE COULD BE ON THE HOOK FOR MURDER IF THE PERSON HE BEAT UP DIES.

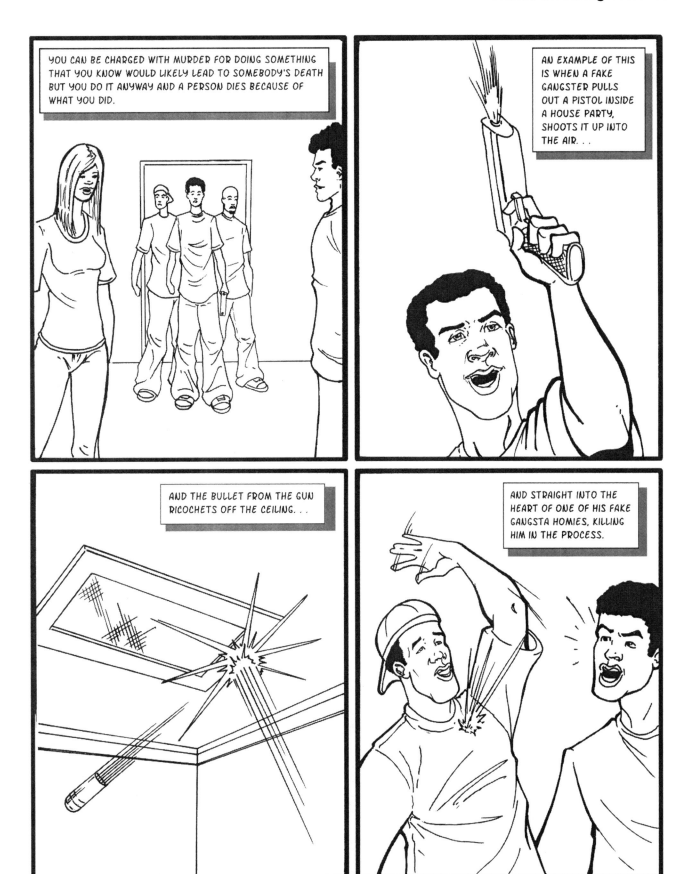

YOU CAN BE CHARGED WITH MURDER FOR DOING SOMETHING THAT YOU KNOW WOULD LIKELY LEAD TO SOMEBODY'S DEATH BUT YOU DO IT ANYWAY AND A PERSON DIES BECAUSE OF WHAT YOU DID.

AN EXAMPLE OF THIS IS WHEN A FAKE GANGSTER PULLS OUT A PISTOL INSIDE A HOUSE PARTY, SHOOTS IT UP INTO THE AIR. . .

AND THE BULLET FROM THE GUN RICOCHETS OFF THE CEILING. . .

AND STRAIGHT INTO THE HEART OF ONE OF HIS FAKE GANGSTA HOMIES, KILLING HIM IN THE PROCESS.

the next time somebody "sets you off." If you kill somebody who provoked you, the fact that you were provoked won't help you very much; you'll still end up in prison.

Involuntary Manslaughter

An unintentional killing that results from doing something risky that you should have known could result in somebody's death is *involuntary manslaughter*. There are two types of involuntary manslaughter: misdemeanor (or unlawful act) manslaughter and criminally negligent manslaughter. A misdemeanor is a crime punishable by up to a year in jail. Misdemeanors are usually less-serious crimes (such as shoplifting under a certain dollar amount). Misdemeanor manslaughter occurs when a person is committing a misdemeanor and somebody gets killed in the process or as a result. Pages 30 and 31 illustrate an example of misdemeanor manslaughter.

In the example, Malcolm had no intention of killing his neighbor. But, he was intentionally slinging rocks at this neighbor's wind chime—the misdemeanor crime of destruction of property. Unfortunately, Malcolm ended up killing his neighbor in the process of destroying the property and likely will be charged with misdemeanor or unlawful act manslaughter. While the slingshot example might seem a little extreme and highly unlikely, just know that crazy things can and do happen when you get involved in criminal activity.

Criminally negligent manslaughter is more difficult to define but usually involves the perpetrator doing something he or she should know is risky or doing something with much less care than the average person would, and somebody else ends up dead because of it. A classic example of involuntary manslaughter is when somebody is goofing around with his friends with a loaded gun. If the gun goes off and kills one of his friends, the guy who was playing with the gun will probably be charged with criminally negligent manslaughter. The only reason he wouldn't be charged with murder is because he didn't intend to kill his friend.

To Sum Up

Understand that you can be charged with assault and battery for instigating a fight. All homicide crimes are serious business and usually carry very stiff penalties if you're found guilty of committing them. Taking another person's life is one of the worst things that you can do because a life cannot be replaced.

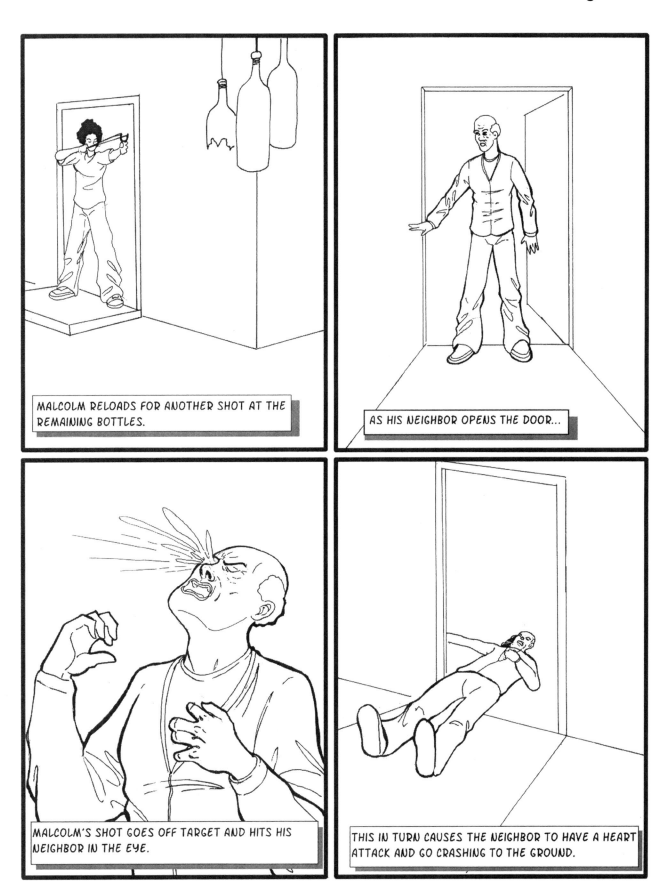

MALCOLM RELOADS FOR ANOTHER SHOT AT THE REMAINING BOTTLES.

AS HIS NEIGHBOR OPENS THE DOOR...

MALCOLM'S SHOT GOES OFF TARGET AND HITS HIS NEIGHBOR IN THE EYE.

THIS IN TURN CAUSES THE NEIGHBOR TO HAVE A HEART ATTACK AND GO CRASHING TO THE GROUND.

CHAPTER RECAP
Concept Review of Chapter 4

- You can be charged with assault if you attempt to use unwanted and/or unlawful force on or against people that results in harm to them.

- You can be charged with assault if you make people feel that you are going to cause them immediate physical harm.

- Using a weapon or dangerous object to assault someone is called aggravated assault.

- You can be charged with battery if you use unlawful and/or unwanted force on someone.

- Giving somebody unwanted physical contact can get you charged with battery.

- Using a weapon or dangerous object to batter someone can lead to a charge of aggravated battery.

- A homicide is the killing of a human being by another person.

- Murder involves intentionally killing someone.

- A killing can be considered intentional if you plan and plot out killing someone and then carry out the plan, resulting in the person's death.

- A killing can be considered intentional if you do something that is so dangerous and/or risky that the chance of someone getting killed is very high, but you do the act anyway and it actually does lead to someone's death.

- Voluntary manslaughter is a homicide that results when people who originally had no intent to kill become provoked by rage, terror, or some other strong emotion. This provocation causes them to "lose it," which in turn causes them to kill before they have time to cool down.

- Involuntary manslaughter is an unintentional killing of a human being by another human being.

- Misdemeanor or unlawful act manslaughter is a form of involuntary manslaughter where a killing happens in the process of or as a result of someone committing a misdemeanor.

- Criminally negligent manslaughter usually involves the perpetrator doing something he or she should know is risky or doing something with much less care than the average person would, resulting in someone's death.

THINK ABOUT IT
Reflection #4

Why is it important to avoid using violence against people? What are some ways to solve problems without using violence?

_____

_____

_____

_____

_____

_____

_____

_____

_____

_____

_____

_____

_____

Chapter 5
Halfway Crimes

IMPORTANT WORDS
Inchoate Crimes
Solicitation
Attempt
Conspiracy
Snitching

The next three crimes that will be discussed are easy to commit because they don't involve doing much. Trying to talk somebody else into committing a crime, or simply agreeing to commit a crime, or even just preparing to commit a crime is enough to get you charged. Forget about having to do anything full blown. In fact, you can even chicken out before going through with the crime and still be on the hook. The fancy name for these crimes is *inchoate crimes*. Inchoate means incomplete. This is why this book also refers to them as *halfway crimes*.

Solicitation

Imagine that Carlos has come up with a foolproof way to break into some guy's car and steal the stereo and speakers, but he doesn't want to risk getting caught himself. He tells his friend, Juan, how to break in without getting caught and asks him to steal the stereo and speakers. He also tells Juan that he'll pay him $100 and that he'll even let him keep the guy's amplifiers for himself.

Without doing anything else, Carlos has just committed a crime. That's right, before they even pick a day for Juan to actually steal the stereo, even before Juan gives him an answer about doing the heist, Carlos has committed the crime of *solicitation*. Basically, if you ask, encourage, hire, or command somebody to commit a crime, you've committed the crime of solicitation.

Solicitation is one of the easiest crimes to commit. In fact, you might have committed this crime a few times yourself without even knowing it. Have you ever walked up to the counter at your local McDonald's, saw a friend from school working the register, and asked her to "hook you up" with some free fries or an extra chicken sandwich? Well, the moment the words came out of your mouth, you committed the crime of solicitation. The friend at the register didn't have to say yes, she didn't even have to actually hear you. Just asking her to hook you up was unlawful. Asking for free stuff from people who don't have the right to give it to you is solicitation because you're really asking them to steal for you.

Attempt

It is a crime to try to commit a crime. For example, trying to steal money is a crime

even if you never actually get your hands on the money. Trying to poison somebody by putting antifreeze in his food is a crime even if he doesn't actually eat the food. *Attempt* is the inchoate crime of trying to commit a crime. Besides simply trying to commit a crime, gathering materials or people together to commit a crime can also be classified as attempt.

To clarify what types of things are considered attempting to commit a crime, read the examples on pages 38–41.

Example 1 on pages 38–39 shows something that is a clear attempt to commit a crime. It's true that Malcolm didn't actually rob the bank. He left empty-handed—but, he attempted to rob the bank, so he's still likely to end up in prison all the same.

Example 2 on pages 40–41 is a variation that is not as clear-cut an attempt, but it is an attempt to commit a crime nonetheless! While there is a small chance it matters that Malcolm decided not to go through with it and was headed home, all the things he did in preparation of his robbery attempt will also matter. The jury will likely look at all he did and think, "This guy is a good-for-nothing thug who should be locked away from society." As a result, they will find him guilty of attempted robbery and do just that—have him locked away from society.

Conspiracy

It's likely you have heard the word conspiracy before. It's often used in reference to a secret and sinister government plan to do something to citizens. That's not the type of conspiracy we want to discuss in this book. In the criminal law context, conspiracy is a special crime. There are two very important things to understand about conspiracy: first, it is one of the most effective tools the police and the prosecution use to put people in prison and, second, it doesn't require the involvement of a mastermind or a complex plan.

Conspiracy is defined as an agreement between two or more people to commit a crime or to help commit a crime. In some states, in order to be convicted of conspiracy, you have to attempt to do at least some part of the crime. But there are some states where all you have to do is agree and you can be convicted of conspiracy. That agreement can be given by voice, such as simply saying yes, or it can be a nonverbal action, such as nodding your head.

See Example 3 on pages 42–44 about Malcolm, Carlos, Zeb, and Rob to learn how conspiracy works.

A very special thing about conspiracy is that every person involved in one can get charged and convicted for the crime of conspiracy and for each crime that was committed to accomplish the goal of the conspiracy. In Example 3, Malcolm, Carlos, Zeb, and Rob will all be charged with conspiracy. They'll also each be charged with grand theft auto for the stolen U-Haul even though only one of them stole the truck.

Example 4 is another, less-complicated example of conspiracy so you don't fall into the trap of thinking it takes a whole lot of players and a clever scheme.

Looking at Example 4, you should be able to recognize where the conspiracy started.

(continued on page 47)

EXAMPLE 1.

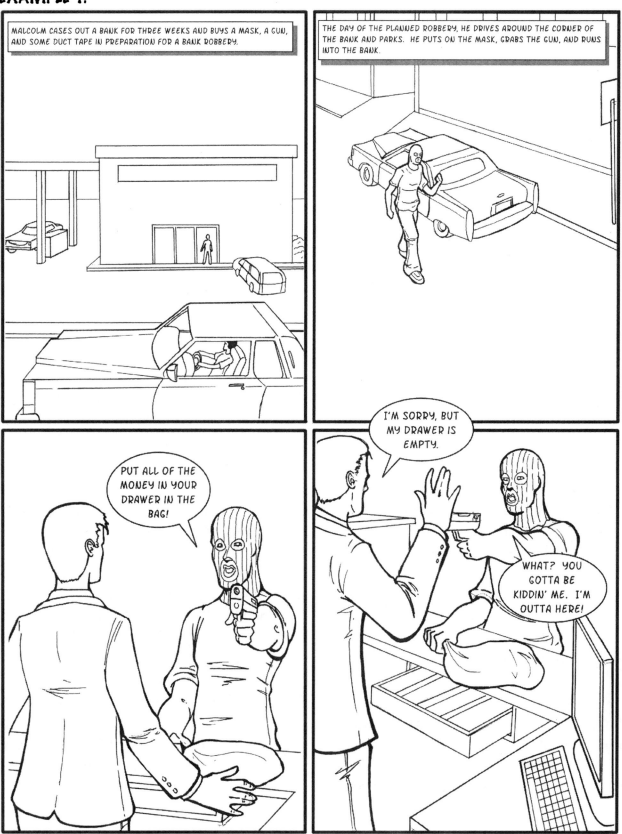

EXAMPLE 2.

THIS TIME MALCOLM DOES ALL OF THE SAME STUFF IN PREPARATION OF THE BANK ROBBERY (BUYING THE MASK, GUN AND DUCT TAPE).

AND JUST LIKE IN THE FIRST EXAMPLE, HE DRIVES AROUND TO THE BACK OF THE BANK AND PARKS, PUTS THE MASK ON, GRABS THE GUN, GETS OUT OF THE CAR, AND HEADS TOWARD THE BANK DOORS.

BUT THIS TIME, BEFORE HE EVEN GETS TO THE DOORS...

HE CHICKENS OUT AND DECIDES NOT TO GO THROUGH WITH THE ROBBERY.

SO HE TAKES OFF THE MASK...

OPENS HIS CAR DOOR...

AND PREPARES TO DRIVE HOME.

SUDDENLY OUT OF NOWHERE, MALCOLM IS SURROUNDED BY THE COPS. THEY YELL AT HIM TO GET HIS SORRY BUTT OUT OF THE VEHICLE.

THEY THEN HANDCUFF AND ARREST HIM FOR ATTEMPTED ARMED ROBBERY.

BUT I DIDN'T EVEN GO IN! HOW COULD I ATTEMPT TO ROB THE BANK IF I DIDN'T GO IN?!

TURNS OUT, AFTER HAVING BEEN TIPPED OFF ABOUT HIS CASING THE BANK, OFFICERS PETTI AND GRIMES STARTING INVESTIGATING MALCOLM'S ACTIVITIES, NOTING HOW OFTEN HE SCOPED OUT THE BANK. THEY ALSO HAD RECORDS OF HIS PURCHASES OF THE GUN, THE MASK, AND THE DUCT TAPE.

THEY PEEPED HIM LEAVING HIS HOUSE WITH ALL OF THAT STUFF IN HAND ON THE DAY OF THE PLANNED ROBBERY. TAILING HIM AT A DISTANCE, THEY PARKED AND WAITED. AT FIRST THEY WERE GOING TO NAB HIM AS HE GOT NEAR THE DOORS BUT NOTICED HIM TURNING BACK AND DECIDED TO ARREST HIM ONCE HE GOT INTO HIS CAR.

EXAMPLE 3.

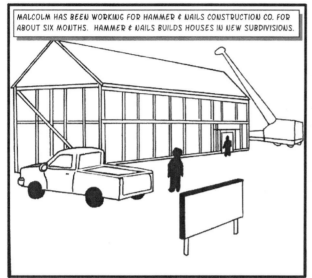

MALCOLM HAS BEEN WORKING FOR HAMMER & NAILS CONSTRUCTION CO. FOR ABOUT SIX MONTHS. HAMMER & NAILS BUILDS HOUSES IN NEW SUBDIVISIONS.

MALCOLM HAS KEYS TO A LOT OF THE HOUSES THAT ARE BEING CONSTRUCTED. HE ALSO HAS THE WORK SCHEDULE SO HE KNOWS WHEN HIS SUPERVISORS WON'T BE AROUND THE HOUSES.

SO HE COMES UP WITH A "BRILLIANT" IDEA TO MAKE SOME MONEY WHILE AT THE SAME TIME KEEPING SUSPICION OFF HIMSELF.

LISTEN, CARLOS, ALL YOU GOTTA DO IS GO INTO THE HOUSES AND SCOOP THE APPLIANCES OUT WHILE ME AND THE CONSTRUCTION CREW ARE WORKING AT A DIFFERENT SITE.

NO DOUBT! GIMME THE KEYS AND LET ME KNOW WHEN YOU AND THE CREW WON'T BE AROUND. MY BOY, ROB, CAN FENCE THE STUFF ON THE STREETS FOR US ONCE WE GET IT OUT.

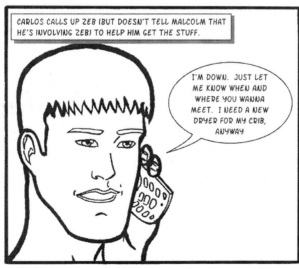

CARLOS CALLS UP ZEB (BUT DOESN'T TELL MALCOLM THAT HE'S INVOLVING ZEB) TO HELP HIM GET THE STUFF.

I'M DOWN. JUST LET ME KNOW WHEN AND WHERE YOU WANNA MEET. I NEED A NEW DRYER FOR MY CRIB, ANYWAY

UNFORTUNATELY, THEY HAVE A "SMALL" PROBLEM.

YO, ZEB, I DON'T THINK MY TRUCK'S BIG ENOUGH TO HAUL THE STUFF.

NO PROBLEM, I KNOW WHAT TO DO.

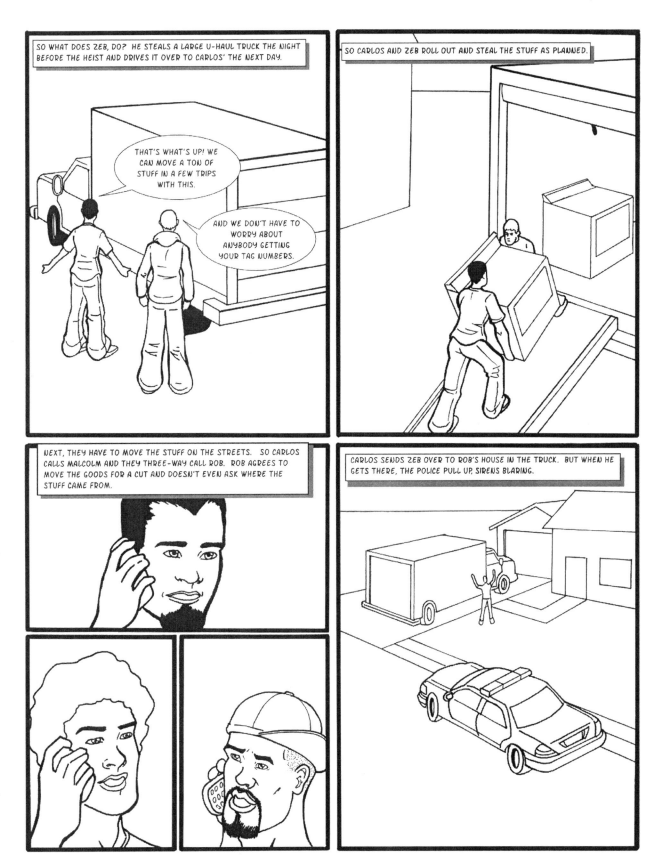

SEE, MALCOLM'S SUPERVISOR THOUGHT MALCOLM WAS SHADY SINCE HIS FIRST DAY OF WORK. HE KEPT A CLOSE EYE ON MALCOLM AND SOMEHOW GOT WIND OF HIS PLAN

HE NOTIFIED OFFICERS GRIMES AND PETTI AND THEY SET UP CAMERAS IN THE TARGET HOUSES. AFTER WATCHING THE SURVEILLANCE TAPES FROM THE HOUSES AND SEEING CARLOS IN THEM THEY CAMP OUT AT ROB'S HOUSE WAITING FOR ZEB TO SHOW UP TO GIVE ROB THE STOLEN GOODS.

THEY KNEW THAT CARLOS WAS COOL WITH ROB, WHO THEY HAD ARRESTED BEFORE FOR SELLING STOLEN GOODS. ONCE ZEB SHOWS UP TO GIVE ROB THE STOLEN STUFF, OFFICERS GRIMES AND PETTI ARREST HIM AND ROB. AND THEY GET ARREST WARRANTS FOR MALCOLM AND CARLOS

SO **EVERYBODY** INVOLVED EVENTUALLY GETS ARRESTED AND TAKEN TO THE STATION.

EXAMPLE 4.

MALCOLM HAS HAD BEEF WITH JON-JON SINCE LAST YEAR WHEN JON-JON TRIED TO HOLLER AT HIS GIRL, ASHLEY, AT THEIR HIGH SCHOOL GRADUATION PARTY. LIKE A PUNK, JON-JON TRIED TO PUSH UP ON ASHLEY WHILE MALCOLM WASN'T AROUND.

IT'S A YEAR LATER AND MALCOLM IS STILL KICKIN' IT WITH ASHLEY.

WANTING TO CHECK OUT HIS HOMEY CARLOS SKOOL SOME FOOLS ON THE COURT, MALCOLM AND ASHLEY ROLL UP TO ONE OF CARLOS' SUMMER BASKETBALL LEAGUE GAMES.

AS MALCOLM AND ASHLEY ARE GOING UP THE BLEACHERS TO FIND SOME SEATS, THAT FOOL, JON-JON, WHO'S SITTING ON THE BOTTOM ROW, TRIES TO GRAB ASHLEY'S ARM TO TALK TO HER—AS IF MALCOLM WASN'T RIGHT THERE WITH HER!

IT'S TIME TO CLAP THIS FOOL. HE GRABBED MY GIRL'S ARM IN FRONT OF ME LIKE I WAS A SUCKER OR SOMETHING.

JON-JON'S DISRESPECT GETS MALCOLM HEATED AND HE DECIDES THAT ENOUGH IS ENOUGH. AT HALFTIME, MALCOLM GOES INTO THE LOCKER ROOM TO LET CARLOS KNOW WHAT WENT DOWN.

YOU GONNA HELP ME OR WHAT?

YOU KNOW I GOT YOU. JUST WAIT UNTIL THE NEXT DEAD BALL SO I CAN GET MY BAT.

(continued from page 37)

Malcolm asked Carlos to help him beat up Jon-Jon. Carlos agreed to help Malcolm. And there you have the conspiracy. No complex plot was needed. The plan was simply to team up and beat up another guy.

Suppose that one of the guys ended up stabbing and killing Jon-Jon in the midst of the beat-down that they were giving him. Both guys would be charged with the killing even though only one of them actually caused Jon-Jon's death. This is something to think about if you and some friends decide to jump somebody. The one crazy individual in your crew who always takes things too far could end up putting everybody on the hook for murder or manslaughter.

Snitching

Once you've agreed to be part of a conspiracy, there's really only one way out, and that is to snitch on your co-conspirators. It's not enough to tell your co-conspirators that "you're out." No, you have to go a step further and try to stop them from committing the crime. This *snitching* usually entails calling the police and warning them about the crime before your co-conspirators commit it.

Snitching also comes into play after a crime is committed. Let's say you stay in the conspiracy and you and your co-conspirators get caught. Once you're caught, the prosecutor will usually separate everybody involved and ask each person to snitch on the others. The prosecutor usually offers the first to snitch a lighter sentence or even a promise to skip prosecuting him. To snitch or not to snitch—that is the question. There's a saying that there is "no honor among thieves." Never is this truer than when it comes to the issue of snitching. While you might not ever snitch on your co-conspirators, more often than not, they'll snitch on you.

"Not my friends," you say. "Never in a million years would my friends sell me out." Think again; tons of people in prison had co-conspirators who snitched on them. It's not hard to figure out why co-conspirators rat on each other. When the prosecutor starts offering deals, the snitching individual says to herself, "Why should I be loyal to them—we're all crooks, anyway? Besides, they'll probably snitch on me first. Well, I'm not going to be the one to do the most time. I'll talk in exchange for a deal."

You may need to think about whether it makes sense to cover for your fellow criminals. Because while you're respecting a street "honor code," your co-conspirators could be setting you up to take most of the punishment for the crime by snitching on you.

Dangers of Being Involved with Criminals

You can be charged for committing a crime as an accomplice if you associate with someone else who commits a crime. The law will say you are a criminal accomplice if you:

1. Help somebody get ready to commit a crime,

2. Help somebody while they're in the process of committing a crime, or

3. Help somebody escape or avoid being caught after they've committed a crime.

The law can find that you have helped somebody commit a crime in many ways. Helping someone get supplies necessary to commit a crime is one way. Looking out for the police or other authorities so as to alert the criminal if somebody comes is another way. Sometimes it takes very little involvement to end up in serious trouble as an accomplice. A classic case is the girl who is involved with a dope dealer. She may end up with a bunch of years in prison for doing something as simple as dropping off her dope dealer boyfriend at the drug house. Never mind that the house is on her way to the mall so she didn't think it was a big deal to give him a ride. Here's the kicker: she could end up getting convicted as if she was the one dealing drugs.

Example 5 on the next page will help you understand how this situation usually goes down.

Now, in this example Keisha is likely to get charged with conspiracy to distribute drugs or some similar charge. She'll be treated as though she was dealing drugs just like Mike. Never mind that she never sold any drugs. Worst of all, because she isn't really involved in the drug game, she can't snitch on anybody in exchange for a plea deal. On the other hand, Mike, who's been in the drug game for a while now, has plenty of people to give up. And he'll likely rat on those people. The result? Mike will be out in no time while Keisha ends up with a hefty prison sentence. The message here, particularly for the ladies, is that having a relationship with a thug might not be the best decision. You could very well end up behind bars for the stuff that he does.

To Sum Up

It is a bad idea to even begin to do anything criminal. You don't have to go through with a crime to be punished as if you did.

EXAMPLE 5.

BECAUSE THEY KNOW WHAT'S UP WITH THE HOUSE, THEY ALSO KNOW WHEN MIKE IS IN THERE SLANGIN'. SO THEY RAID THE SPOT AND PICK UP EVERYBODY INSIDE, INCLUDING KEISHA.

PETTI AND GRIMES GO ALL THROUGH HER STUFF.

AND END UP FINDING SOME PHONE MESSAGES SHE WROTE DOWN WITH INSTRUCTIONS FOR MIKE FROM HIS DRUG CONTACT.

THAT WAS BAD ENOUGH, BUT WHAT KEISHA DIDN'T KNOW IS THAT THEY HAD PREVIOUSLY TAPED HER DRIVING MIKE TO ANOTHER DOPE SPOT AROUND THE WAY A COUPLE OF TIMES.

PLUS THEY SAW MIKE DROP HER A COUPLE HUNDRED DOLLAR BILLS (MONEY TO GET HER HAIR DONE, OR SOME NEW SHOES SHE'D BEEN WANTING) WHEN HE CAME BACK OUT OF THE OTHER DOPE SPOT.

CHAPTER RECAP
Concept Review of Chapter 5

- The term *inchoate crime* refers to incomplete crimes. Asking others to commit a crime for you, planning to commit a crime with others, and attempting to commit a crime are all inchoate crimes.

- Asking somebody to help you commit a crime is the crime of solicitation.

- It is a crime to attempt to commit a crime.

- You can be charged with the crime of conspiracy if you agree to help somebody commit a crime.

- Once involved in a conspiracy, you can be held responsible for everything anyone else in the conspiracy does.

- In order to free yourself from being responsible for the actions of the other people in a conspiracy, you must actively work to thwart the conspiracy. This means that you will likely have to tell the authorities about the conspiracy before it goes down.

- If you don't snitch on your co-conspirators before they go through with the agreed-upon crime, you will be in trouble along with them.

- Sometimes, once the people involved in a conspiracy are caught, the first person to snitch on the others gets the lightest sentence—or possibly even freedom from prosecution altogether.

- You can be charged as an accomplice to a crime if you help somebody who commits a crime, whether you help them before, during, or after the crime.

THINK ABOUT IT
Reflection #5

What steps can you take to avoid getting into a criminal conspiracy? Do you think snitching is a good thing to do or a bad thing to do? Please explain your answer.

Chapter 6
Sex Crimes

IMPORTANT WORDS
Statutory Rape
Strict Liability Crime
Sexting

Statutory Rape

Every high-school student should be informed about statutory rape. Statutory rape is when a person of a certain age has sex with a person under a certain age—and doing so is not allowed by the law. Unlike rape, statutory rape doesn't have to involve the underage person having sex against his or her will.

Statutory rape is a strict liability crime. A *strict liability crime*, put simply, is a crime where there are no excuses—that is, no reason is a good enough reason to not be charged with a crime. If a law makes an action a strict liability crime, then it doesn't matter what you intended or if you should have or could have known you were committing a crime. Once the thing is done, you can be charged for the crime.

In the case of statutory rape, nothing you say or do can keep you from going to prison if you had sex with an underage person. The fact that she is your girlfriend? No excuse. The fact that he's the one who initiated sex? Also, no excuse. Even mistakenly thinking that he or she was actually an adult is no excuse. In fact, they could have even lied about their age and you would still be held responsible!

In some states, it is statutory rape if a person 17 or older has sex with a person 16 or under. This means that if a 17-year-old senior in high school has a 16-year-old sophomore girlfriend, he could end up behind bars for having sex with her. Not only that, he may also have to register as a sex offender for the rest of his life. He could even eventually marry the girl and still have to register as a sex offender! Fair or not, those are the possible consequences of statutory rape.

Sexting

Cell phones and other information devices are being used by more people than ever before. And while cell phones and computers can be very useful, a dark side to their use exists.

Social networking sites such as Facebook and Twitter allow people to communicate and connect as never before. The whole world seems to be connected and just about anybody can glimpse into other people's lives. With so many reality television shows on, it's common to see people's private moments plastered all over the TV and the Internet for everybody to see.

So you might not think it's a big deal to post revealing pictures of yourself on your Facebook page or to send a sexy picture on your phone to somebody else. In fact, it's likely that you know somebody who's done this before. No big deal, right? Wrong. And there are tons of reasons why.

Let's take a moment to discuss the sending or forwarding of nude or sexually suggestive or explicit pictures on your cell phone, also known as "sexting." Most of the time, *sexting* involves a person sending a picture or pictures to a person who they like or that they're in a relationship with. People sending the pictures usually think that the person receiving the picture will be the only one viewing it.

But that's where they're wrong—especially teens. Girls sending explicit pictures often find out that the recipient has now forwarded the pictures to several friends. And those friends forward them to several of their friends, who forward it to several of their friends, and so on and so on. In a very short time, a lot of strangers know all of the girl's "business." They quickly find out that most horrifying thing about sending and posting things digitally—you have no control over the stuff once it's sent.

You might think that it's okay to post explicit pictures because, after all, you have a great body and you want to show it off, but that's a very shortsighted view. Even though TV makes it seem that showing off your body might possibly lead to fame and fortune, it usually doesn't work that

way. Yes, some people have achieved notoriety by "baring it all" or making sex tapes and the like. In most instances, though, instead of fame, girls only end up with a bad reputation.

Besides, is your body what you really want to be known for? At the end of the day, most people want to be liked and appreciated for who they are—not just for their bodies or physical appearance. But when you promote your body as your only important feature, people will treat you accordingly. They won't want to get to know you on the inside.

But let's look even deeper at the consequences of sexting. As stated earlier, you have no control over pictures that you post or send. And who knows where some of these messages and pictures might end up? What if they make it all the way around to your parents' phones? How embarrassing would that be?

College entrance offices and employers are doing Internet checks on potential students and employees now more than ever. You could find yourself denied your college choice(s) or that job you really wanted, all over a poorly thought-out decision.

In order to protect children from being exploited by people who traffic in child pornography, the government has laws that make it illegal to send and own pornographic pictures of individuals under a certain age. The law is so strict that just having explicit pictures of underage individuals will get you thrown in prison. It doesn't matter how you got them.

The social consequences of sending explicit messages and pictures can be horrific, but even more serious consequences may result—that is, legal consequences. Remember that you should THINK and CARE about the possible consequences of your decisions and actions.

Let's look at how a decision regarding sexting can lead to serious legal consequences:

An underage girl, Julie, takes an explicit picture of herself and sends it to her boyfriend, Fernando, who is also underage. He has an older brother, Jorge, who is 18. To impress Jorge and show him that he's a stud who has his girl sending naked pictures to him, Fernando forwards the picture to Jorge.

Jorge opens the picture file. He doesn't know that having this picture on his phone is a crime. Plus, he thinks it's funny that his little brother has a girl sending naked pictures. He also thinks it would be cool to show his friends how cool Fernando is. So, he sends the picture on to several of his friends with the message: "Yo, check out what my little brother has his girlfriend doing! LOL!"

Eventually, word gets around the school that this picture is circulating among some of the senior boys in the high school. The principal gets wind of it and tracks down a senior who has the picture on his phone. She questions the young man and the young man says that just about everybody in the school has received the picture on their phone.

The principal calls the police and they contact Julie. Now embarrassed that the whole school has seen the picture, Julie tells the investigators that she only sent the picture to her boyfriend, Fernando. When the investigators catch up to Fernando, he says that he only sent the picture to his older brother. The police catch up to Jorge who admits to receiving the picture and forwarding it. When they discover that Jorge is 18, they arrest him for possessing and distributing child pornography.

Jorge goes to trial and is convicted. He gets two years in prison and several years of probation. When he's released from prison, he has to register as a sex offender for the rest of his life and cannot live anywhere near children—all because he received and forwarded pictures on his cell phone.

Prison, probation, and registering as a sex offender for the rest of your life are hefty penalties to pay just for receiving and forwarding a few pictures. Sending and receiving explicit pictures via a computer or cell phone might seem like harmless fun, but the consequences are anything but fun.

To Sum Up

It is extremely important to know the statutory rape laws in your state. Just know that once you've crossed the line with an underage individual, you have put yourself in a situation where you have no excuses.

Technology connects us in ways never imagined and it's hard to deny the amazing communications options that it provides. But you have to be careful about how you use communications technology. Used in the wrong way, it can lead to some harsh legal consequences. So before you send that picture from your phone, THINK and CARE about the consequences of pressing the "send" button.

CHAPTER RECAP
Concept Review of Chapter 6

- A strict liability crime is one in which you will automatically be punished for doing something that the law says not to do—or not doing something that the law requires you to do.

- Statutory rape is a strict liability crime in many states. Statutory rape occurs when a person over a certain age has sexual relations with a person under a certain age.

- Sexting is the sending of sexually explicit or suggestive messages or photographs, usually between mobile phones.

- If you are an adult, simply having naked or semi-naked pictures of an underage person on your phone can lead to a charge of possessing child pornography, regardless of how the pictures got on your phone or who sent them.

- Whatever you send via electronic means can be passed around to a large number of people—some of whom you may not want to view your private messages.

THINK ABOUT IT
Reflection #6

What are the potential consequences of sending inappropriate pictures over the Internet or telephone? What can you do to avoid being charged with a sex crime?

_____

_____

_____

_____

_____

_____

_____

_____

_____

_____

_____

_____

_____

_____

Chapter 7
Bullying

Bullying Generally

A crime that is really hurting school-aged young people far too much today is bullying. *Bullying* is any harm or threat of harm to someone that occurs in connection with school, school activities, functions, and school networks. Bullying also occurs whenever you threaten somebody with harm or harass them and it interferes with their education or their school environment.

Bullying is very serious—and not just because of the punishment you can receive for doing it. Victims of bullying sometimes develop emotional damage that lasts for the rest of their lives. Some students who get bullied aren't able to focus on their school work. Others choose not to participate in school activities because of fear of being bullied. As a result, they get poor grades, struggle to advance to the next grade level, and fall behind. They don't get the chance to explore their talents and abilities. Eventually they may fail to get into college because of poor grades and a transcript that shows a lack of extracurricular activities. Later, they may have problems finding a job.

Bullying is not fun and games. It doesn't show how tough you are, and it doesn't make you any cooler than the people you bully. Anybody can pick on a weaker or smaller person. After the cheap laugh you get from others for picking on someone different, then what? What do you really get for bullying? Nothing important. Nothing good. In fact, a lot of bad things happen as a result of bullying. Did you know that colleges may avoid letting you in if you have a history of bullying? Employers might choose not to hire you because nobody wants a bully working for them. If you are an elementary, middle, or high school student found guilty of bullying, you may be transferred to an alternative school. If you are in high school, you can also be convicted of any underlying crimes committed in the process of bullying. For instance, if you bully somebody by physically attacking him, you could be charged with assault and battery. If you bully somebody by verbally threatening him, you could be charged with making terroristic threats.

Sometimes really tragic things happen as a result of bullying. Some bullying victims have been known to become very depressed and to attempt to kill themselves. Some have succeeded. Could you handle causing someone's death? Is that something that you want eating at you for the rest of your life? So THINK hard about the decision you and your friends make about picking on someone and CARE about all the horrible things that could happen as a result. Choose not to be a bully and show courage by encouraging your friends to stop bullying also.

Cyberbullying

Over forty percent of teenagers with Internet access have reported being bullied online. Fifty-eight percent of students in 4th–8th grade report having mean or cruel things said to them online, and fifty-three percent of those students say that they have bullied someone else online.

What are some ways that kids bully others online? Some common practices are: posting hurtful or embarrassing information about somebody on social networking sites such as Facebook and Twitter; altering photographs through the use of digital editing software to humiliate another person; and recording conversations without the other person's permission and then posting the conversation online.

The moral argument against cyberbullying is that it is downright wrong to do these things to other people. Cyberbullies tend to be cowardly people who often hide behind anonymous screen names. Nobody wants his or her life ruined by some spiteful hiding coward.

One of the biggest problems with posting stuff online is that it can be there forever.

You might be angry with somebody and post something that really hurts that person. Later, you might cool down and really regret what you posted. But it's too late. Now that it's online, it can be forwarded around to hundreds, if not thousands, of people. It may be something that comes up every time potential employers run a background check on that person. As a result, he or she might not be able to find a job. Now you've ruined somebody's life for years to come over some petty fallout. Resorting to cyberbullying to hurt somebody can have long-lasting—and possibly lifelong—implications.

There are criminal implications, as well, to bothering someone through the use of electronic means. Sending constant emails and text messages with the intent to bother, seek revenge on, or threaten somebody is *cyberstalking* and it is a crime.

Even if you have what you think are good intentions, you can still be charged with cyberstalking. For instance, you might think that persistence pays off if you want to gain the attention of the girl or guy you really like. But if you constantly bug that person after he or she has told you to stop emailing, texting, or messaging, you can be charged with cyberstalking. There is even a crime called *harassment by computer*, and it only requires one incident of bothering someone by using a computer to be charged.

Fighting Bullying

Because bullying can result in so many terrible consequences, fighting bullying is very important. The good news is there are lots of ways to do so. The first and easiest thing anyone can do to fight bullying is to decide not to be a bully themselves. If you have an opportunity to pick on someone or make fun of someone, but choose not to, you instantly become a top fighter against bullying. The second thing you can do to fight bullying is report any bullying that is happening to you or someone you know. Go to a teacher, a school administrator, a parent or some other adult you know and feel comfortable with and tell them about the bullying. Don't ever think there is no one you can turn to for help when it comes to bullying. Your parents and school teachers will surprise you with how helpful they can be if you report that you are being bullied. Definitely tell them.

The thing to remember when it comes to the fight against bullying is that it's not easy. It may be hard not join in when your friends are making fun of someone and having fun at the victim's expense. It may be even harder to stand up and tell them to stop. But keep in mind that if you can't stand up to your friends, in a way, you're being bullied. At the very least you're exhibiting cowardice. So be brave and take a stand against bullying.

To Sum Up

You can be thrown out of school and charged with crimes if you bully. Instead of being a bully or being a bystander watching others get bullied, do something about it by reporting it when you see it happening.

CHAPTER RECAP

Concept Review of Chapter 7

- Bullying is any harm or threat of harm to someone that occurs in connection with school, school activities, functions, and school networks.

- If found guilty of bullying, you may be transferred to an alternative school, and can also be convicted of any underlying crimes committed in the bullying.

- Cyberbullying is the malicious use of electronic means—such as the Internet—to bother, harass, or bully people.

- You can be punished for cyberbullying and cyberstalking.

- Things posted online may stay posted forever or they may be very difficult to remove.

- The easiest way to fight bullying is to choose not to be a bully yourself.

- You can fight bullying by reporting to school administrators and parents when you see bullying.

THINK ABOUT IT
Reflection #7

Why is bullying a bad idea and what can you do to fight against bullying?

Chapter 8
Other Criminal Activity to Be Mindful Of

IMPORTANT WORDS
Arson
Terroristic Threats
Destruction of Property
Underage Drinking
Drug Possession
Obstruction of Justice
Disorderly Conduct

The majority of this book deals with serious crimes, but some less-serious activities deserve mention as well. Something that begins small can grow into an out-of-control criminal situation. This section will touch on a few "minor" acts that should be avoided.

Setting Things on Fire

Some kids and teens go through a "fire starter" stage. Most of us come out of this stage with maybe a few minor burns and some scorched items here and there. For some, though, playing with fire leads to tragedy—the loss of a home or someone's life, for example. "Playing with fire" can quickly escalate into *arson*, which is the burning of a home or other building. An arson charge carries severe punishment. Simply put, fire is nothing to play with.

Making Threats

At this point, it should be abundantly clear to you that your mouth can get you into some serious trouble. We've explained how simply saying yes can implicate you in a conspiracy. But that's not the only trouble using your voice can invite. You should also be aware of the pitfalls of verbally threatening others.

Have you ever argued with one of your teachers who refused to listen to your side of the story? And on top of that, she told you to leave the classroom? Well, let's say you're so angry that without thinking you tell the teacher, "I hate you! I'm gonna come back here and blow the school up!" A stupid, offhand remark made in the heat of anger at perceived unfair treatment could be considered a threat to be taken seriously.

In the past, making a threat like the one above would simply be labeled as a kid "blowing off some steam." Not anymore. Today, threats are taken much more seriously. And the person making the threats is treated severely. Threatening to "blow up your school" could be considered a *terroristic threat*. And terroristic threats are handled by law enforcement authorities—not school administrators. In other words, do not expect a slap on the wrist.

Even threatening to confront your teacher after school could land you in jail. In fact, making threats in general is simply not very smart. Very little good comes from threatening other people. Plus, you may be setting yourself up for some unwanted interactions with law enforcement. Keep threats to yourself and find a constructive way to resolve your anger.

Destruction of Property

For the most part, you're allowed to do whatever you want with your own property. However, painting on and trashing public property or someone else's private property is off limits. Would you want someone trashing your property? How would you feel if you came home and found garbage all over your yard or the windows of your home bashed in?

Destroying other people's property is wrong—plain and simple. More importantly, it's illegal. In some cases, you can be charged with a felony for destroying someone's property, depending on the extent of the damage you caused. And while damaging property isn't as bad as causing damage to a human being, courts take *the destruction of property* very seriously. Most people work hard to buy nice things, and judges and juries recognize this and will punish you accordingly.

Underage Drinking

Drinking alcohol should be avoided until you are of legal drinking age. Alcohol impairs brain functions, and it's actually listed as a poison (ethanol). Considering that many adults have a difficult time handling alcohol, it should go without saying that underage individuals are definitely not equipped to drink alcohol and function normally. Possession of alcohol by a minor is usually a crime in and of itself. And if it was found that your parents gave you the alcohol or

made it easy for you to get your hands on their alcohol, they may end up going to jail.

Further, drinking and driving is a major problem among teens. Drinking and driving is a volatile mix because most teens have extremely limited experience behind the wheel. Add to that the mentally impaired state that alcohol induces and you have a recipe for tragedy. If you hit and kill someone because you were under the influence of alcohol while driving, you could end up with a manslaughter charge, which means you'll likely be sentenced to time in either juvenile detention or prison.

Drug Possession and Being Around Drug Users

Almost everybody knows that you can be put away for selling drugs. But did you know that you can get in a lot of trouble just for having a small amount of personal-use drugs on you? You can be charged with *drug possession*. Even being around people who have drugs on them—even if you don't have any on you—can lead to your being arrested.

Obstruction and Disorderly Conduct

While it may not always be in your best interest to answer all questions that police pose to you, it *is* in your best interest to be polite and respectful toward the cops. Being disrespectful and difficult with the police can result in a charge of *obstruction of justice* or *disorderly conduct*. *Obstruction* is the interference, through words or actions, with the proper operations of a court or officers of the court. Police officers are officers of the court. Obstruction, in other words, means getting in the way of officers doing their jobs.

Disorderly conduct is any act that disturbs the peace or endangers the morals, health, or safety of a community.

Just as some people are nice and others are not, police officers are no different. You're going to have nice ones and some who are not so nice. Regardless of how the police act toward you, it is your job to remain respectful and calm toward them.

Of course, this is easier said than done. Some police officers really know how to push people's buttons and to rile them, causing an individual to act belligerently toward them. Usually the individual starts yelling or cursing at the police, which is also accompanied by animated body movements that the police perceive as threatening. This, in turn, causes the police to act in an aggressive manner. You should know that when the police feel that they're being challenged,

they will move swiftly and forcefully to get the situation under control. This could result in your being physically subdued in a violent way. Plus, you'll probably get arrested for disorderly conduct or obstruction of justice.

Is deciding to give the police a piece of your mind really worth the consequences? Probably not. So take a deep breath and calm yourself whenever you are interacting with the police. Keep your cool no matter what the police say to you. Later chapters of this book will discuss in detail how to conduct yourself appropriately with the police.

To Sum Up

Be mindful of "little" things you do that you may think are harmless but that can grow into criminal situations. Again, it is important to THINK and CARE constantly about your actions and the resulting consequences.

CHAPTER RECAP
Concept Review of Chapter 8

- Setting things on fire can lead you to be charged with arson (intentionally and illegally setting fire to a structure or land).

- You can be charged with a crime for threatening to do serious damage to people or property.

- You can be charged with a crime for defacing or trashing public property or other people's private property.

- You can be charged with a crime for consuming alcohol if you are not of legal drinking age.

- If you cause someone's death because you were drinking while driving, you may be charged with manslaughter.

- Being disrespectful and/or belligerent with the police may lead you to be charged with disorderly conduct or obstruction of justice.

THINK ABOUT IT
Reflection #8

Choose one of the activities covered in Chapter 8 (fire starting, making threats, destroying property, underage drinking, etc.) and discuss how engaging in that activity can turn into a very serious situation.

Chapter 9
Excuses and Justifications

IMPORTANT WORDS
Affirmative Legal Defenses
Mistake of Fact
Duress
Self-Defense
Unlawful Force

The previous pages of this book have discussed several different ways in which you can commit crimes, some intentionally and some carelessly. It may seem like you're pretty much in danger for tons of things that you may do on a weekly, if not daily, basis. But there is some good news. In some situations, the law allows for special excuses and justifications that allow you to avoid being punished by the criminal justice system.

These excuses and justifications are known as affirmative legal defenses. We'll just call them legal defenses going forward. The legal defenses that will be discussed in this chapter are:

1. Mistake of Fact,

2. Duress, and

3. Self-Defense and Defense of Others.

Mistake of Fact

As imperfect human beings, we all have times when we see, hear, or understand something incorrectly and then act on that incorrect perception. The law actually makes allowances for times when that incorrect perception or faulty information causes us to do something that's normally considered criminal. When we end up committing a crime based on having our facts wrong, the law sometimes lets us off the hook.

Here's an example to help you understand this concept better:

It's hunting season and Rob is legally hunting for deer in the woods. He hears a rustle in the bramble and sees something brown and large quickly dart across the woods in the distance. Without hesitation, he raises his rifle and fires in the direction of the movement.

Bang! Down goes the creature. Seeing the animal lying still, as if frozen, Rob makes his way toward it. Now, within a few feet from the dead animal, he fixes his eyes on its carcass. And what he sees makes his blood run cold.

The "animal" he killed isn't a buck, but a man wearing a brown jacket!

In the above scenario, is there any indication that Rob intended to kill a person? No. He believed that he was shooting at a deer in an area where deer roamed and during a time and location in which it was legally permissible to hunt for deer.

Rob made what's known as a *mistake of fact*. He was enjoying a legal activity (hunting during hunting season), but because of his incorrect perception, he ended up doing something that is usually considered illegal—in this case, killing another human being for no good reason. But, because his perception of the facts was wrong, Rob probably won't be convicted of a crime. This makes sense because he never intended to kill anybody and he wasn't acting carelessly or recklessly.

An important point to remember when it comes to the mistake of fact defense is that you cannot be in the process of doing anything unlawful. For instance, let's say Oscar sneaks up on Paul and punches him in the back of the head, but it turns out that the person he thought was Paul was really Tom. Unfortunately for Oscar, he won't be let off the hook even though he mistakenly punched the wrong guy. This is because Oscar was doing something unlawful. Can you guess what it was? The answer is that he was committing battery (using unlawful force) on another person. As you've learned in earlier chapters of this book, battery is a crime. Because Oscar was engaged in illegal activity, he can't use the mistake of fact defense and will have to answer for punching Tom. In other words, it won't matter that he mistakenly punched the wrong person. Even

if he had decked the "right" person, Paul, he still would have been committing a crime.

Duress

One of the strongest defenses available to a person accused of a crime is the excuse that he or she was forced to commit the crime—usually under threat of some type of violence. In other words, the crime was committed under *duress*. The duress excuse comes with a very important exception and it is this: you cannot use this defense to avoid punishment for killing another human being. Even if somebody held a gun to your head with instructions to kill somebody else for them, you will still be punished if you carry out the orders.

The duress excuse usually only works with crimes involving property, such as larceny and burglary. So if somebody threatened to harm you if you didn't steal for them, you may be able to avoid punishment by making your attorney aware that you committed it under duress.

Self-defense

Self-defense is probably the best-known legal defense, and rightly so because of its roots in one of the most basic principles of the animal kingdom—survival. "Get them before they get you" is a way of life for many wild creatures. Luckily for us, such situations are rare in the human world, but they do come up from time to time. At some point in your life, you may be faced with a situation where you have no choice but to hurt somebody else to keep them from hurting you or your loved ones.

This is where the excuse of self-defense comes in. It allows you to legally hurt or even use deadly force on somebody who might seriously hurt or kill you. The general rule is that you can use force against someone else if you believe it's the only way to protect yourself against that person's use of unlawful and immediate violence against you.

First, to even begin to have a legitimate self-defense argument, you have to reasonably believe somebody is attacking you with unlawful force. That means if the average person wouldn't have thought that the force you were facing was unlawful, your defense doesn't have a chance. An example of unlawful force is when somebody comes up to you and tries to hit you for no reason.

Second, if you attack somebody when you don't really believe that it is necessary to protect yourself, and then try to claim self-defense, you will not win. You actually have to believe that force is necessary to protect yourself against the other person's force against you; otherwise, you'll be charged with battery, or even murder if you use deadly force.

Third, you have to be careful with the amount of force you use to defend yourself. You can only use as much force as is necessary to defend yourself. That means if someone is about to knuckle you up, and you can stop them with your hands, you can't pick up a pole or pull out a gun. However, if the only way you can stop someone from using unlawful force against you is to use a pole or gun that you are in lawful possession of, you can do so.

Finally, you cannot be reckless in your self-defense. You still have to be careful not to accidentally hurt an innocent bystander when you are defending yourself. Otherwise

you will find yourself in trouble with the law for the harm you caused to the bystander.

Defending Other People

At some point, you may find yourself defending one of your friends from violence. And just as with self-defense, there are rules for *defending others*. The rules pretty much mirror those for self-defense. The person you're defending has to be facing unlawful and immediate violence. Any force you use can't be excessive. And you cannot be reckless.

Protecting Your Personal Property

You also have a right to *protect your personal property* by using force. But are the rules pretty much the same as protecting yourself and others? Are they different when it comes to stuff instead of people? The answer is that some rules are the same, and some are different.

It's important to remember when protecting your property that property is just things—things that are not equal to a human life. This means that the person trying to take your property is more valuable than your property. Yes, the person might be total scum who hasn't ever done a positive thing in his or her entire life, but in the eyes of the law, any life is more valuable than your stuff.

Why is it important that you realize a life—even a seemingly worthless person's life—is more important than your property? It's important so that you don't get the idea that it's okay to take somebody's life just to protect your things.

It is not okay to use deadly force to keep somebody from taking your property. It doesn't matter if it's a diamond-and-platinum watch, that you spent three years working overtime every week to buy. If your life is not in danger, you cannot use deadly force to keep the person from taking your stuff. Now, some states allow you to pull out a weapon (assuming you can legally possess and carry it) and direct it at the person trying to take your property, which might cause him or her to rethink robbing you. Even in those states, though, you can't actually use deadly force; you can only threaten to use it.

If your life is not in danger, and you take somebody's life just to keep him or her from taking your property, you'll be in serious trouble. In fact, depending on the state that you live in, you could possibly be put to death. Being put to death because you tried to keep somebody from *taking* your property hardly seems worth it.

Let's go through the rules that apply when it comes to protecting your property. The first rule is that you can only use force to keep other people from taking your property. Once they've taken your stuff and had it for a while, you can't use any kind of force to take your stuff back. Instead, you're supposed to go to the authorities (whether school or legal authorities) and seek their assistance with getting your stolen stuff back.

Second, you can only use as much force as is necessary to keep the person from taking your property. At this point, you should understand that you always have to be careful with how much force you use, whether defending yourself, other people, or your property.

The rules regarding protecting your property differ slightly when it comes to your home. You're usually allowed to use deadly force to protect your home, but only if the person(s) breaking in pose(s) an immediate threat of serious bodily harm or death to the people inside. It's not usually that hard to convince the police that the invader posed a danger to the people inside. Most of the time, when people try to break into somebody else's house, they're considered dangerous.

Still, keep in mind that it is usually a bad idea to use deadly force on the invader if he or she is clearly leaving the house and is no longer a threat. If you shoot someone in the back as he or she is leaving, you could be charged with murder.

To Sum Up

There are certain legal excuses and justifications that you can use to avoid government punishment for doing things that you would otherwise be punished for. But these excuses and justifications can only be used in very special circumstances. They usually won't be of much help if you intended to do something unlawful in the first place.

CHAPTER RECAP
Concept Review of Chapter 9

- In certain situations, the law may accept special excuses and justifications that allow you to avoid punishment for doing something that would otherwise be considered a crime.

- You can use the mistake of fact defense if you had no intention of doing anything unlawful, but because you perceived something incorrectly, ended up doing something unlawful.

- You can use force to protect yourself against any unlawful force being used against you.

- You must be careful not to use more force than is necessary to protect yourself.

- Deadly force can only be used when somebody is using or threatening to immediately use deadly force on you.

- Force can be used to keep someone from taking your things. However, deadly force cannot be used to keep someone from taking your things if you are not in danger of great bodily harm or death.

- Deadly force can be used to protect yourself and everyone in your home if someone breaks in posing a threat to the lives of those inside. However, you usually cannot use deadly force if the invader is retreating.

THINK ABOUT IT
Reflection #9

Are the rules of self-defense what you thought they were before you read Chapter 9? If so, in what ways? If not, in what ways do they differ from what you believed before reading Chapter 9?

Chapter 10

Getting in Trouble for Doing Nothing

IMPORTANT WORDS
Crime of Omission
Duty

We've seen so far that the law punishes you for your actions. On the flip side, sometimes the law punishes you for failing to act. In other words, you can find yourself in trouble for doing NOTHING! A crime for which you can be punished because you didn't do something that you should have done is called a *crime of omission*.

Outside of common decency, most of us probably don't think we have an obligation to help others. And there are tons of stories of people standing around offering no help while someone was being beaten, with no punishments given out to them. In most cases, you don't have to help anybody out of a dangerous situation if you don't want to. But sometimes you do. It all depends on whether you have a *duty* to help the person, which in turn depends on the specific situation.

The following is a list of rules and situations explaining when you have a duty to help another person in danger:

- **When You Have a Special Relationship to the Person or People**: Parents and older family members are expected to help their children and younger family members out of immediate, dangerous, and life-threatening situations, if they can do so without making things worse. The same goes for husbands and wives. In some instances, even bosses and employees have to help each other when one or the other is in immediate, serious danger.

- **When a Law Requires You to Help**: Some states have laws that require the people who caused a car accident to help the people injured in the accident, provided they can do so without making things worse. Some cities have "Good Samaritan" laws that require citizens to help strangers in serious danger—again, provided it can be done without making things worse.

- **When You Have a Contractual Obligation to Help**: Nurses have to help the sick and elderly people they're being paid to provide care for. Lifeguards have to help swimmers at the beaches and pools where they're working. Babysitters must help the children they're watching. In these situations, the people's jobs require providing help to their clients or customers. Failure to do so could mean more than just getting fired. It could mean prison time.

- **If You Caused the Problem in the First Place**: If you do something to somebody—even a complete stranger—that puts them in serious danger or in a life-threatening situation, you are usually required to help them out of that situation.

- **If You Became Involved in a Situation and Tried to Help Somebody in Danger**: If you find somebody in a dangerous situation that you didn't

cause and you begin helping that person, you now have a responsibility to continue helping him or her provided your help doesn't make the situation worse. According to the law, you can't leave somebody in a worse position than when you found the person once you jump in to help.

To Sum Up

Rarely will you be required to help somebody when they are in a dangerous situation. However, in some situations you do have an obligation to help. It's important that you understand when you are obligated to help somebody out of a dangerous situation so that you don't get punished for failing to do anything.

CHAPTER RECAP
Concept Review of Chapter 10

- Sometimes, the law requires you to help people. If you fail to offer help, you could be punished.

- Failure to do something that the law requires you to do is called an act of omission.

- Whether you can be charged with a crime for not helping somebody depends upon whether you have a duty to help the person.

- You may have a duty to help a person who is in immediate danger depending on the situation, or your relationship to the person, or whether a law requires you to help the person. Sometimes you may have a duty to help based on a combination of these factors.

THINK ABOUT IT
Reflection #10

Can you think of any situations that you have been in or seen that could have resulted in criminal charges for not doing something? Please explain. How can you avoid finding yourself in trouble with the law for not doing something?

Part I Recap and Lessons Learned

Now that you have learned some important information about criminal law, let's review some of the most important points.

- You don't have to be a "bad" person to be a criminal. Doing things that the government punishes you for doing is what makes you a criminal. It's that simple.

- Claiming that you didn't know you were doing anything wrong rarely keeps you out of trouble when you break the law. You'll be in trouble if you should have known what you were doing was something that the government considers a crime or criminal activity. It's your job to recognize when situations are suspicious or could place you in a criminal situation.

- You should always be THINKING and CARING about your actions and the consequences of those actions. Being careless or reckless can lead to the injury or death of others, which can then lead to your being severely punished by the government.

- Getting into fights and handling things through the use of violence can often lead to criminal charges. Taking what doesn't belong to you, especially by force or threatening force, is a quick way to the state pen.

- Using technology to bully or harass people is not just morally wrong—it is a crime.

- It is very easy to become involved in criminal activity. Asking somebody to "hook you up" with free stuff or just agreeing with your friends to do illegal activities may not seem like a big deal. But as you've learned, even these minimal, seemingly harmless activities can land you behind bars.

- Being involved with people who commit crimes is also something that you should seriously reconsider. Remember that you may find yourself in trouble because of their activities.

It's all about choices. The choices you make can have a deep effect on the course of your future. One bad choice can ruin your life. All of your hopes, dreams, and aspirations could end in a prison cell. The previous chapters should have given you something to think about and should encourage you to use good judgment so that you don't find yourself ensnared in the criminal justice system.

Of course, even if you've done all the right things and honestly tried to avoid having run-ins with law enforcement, you might still find yourself confronted by the police. It's important that you know that you have rights that help protect you from being unfairly victimized by the police. Part II of *When the Cops Come Knockin'* explains your rights when dealing with law enforcement. Read on—your freedom might depend on it.

REVIEW OF PART I

Directions

In the lines provided below, discuss two major lessons that you learned in the first part of this book.

PART II

YOUR RIGHTS WHEN DEALING WITH THE POLICE

Chapter 11
You Have Rights

At some point in your life, you're probably going to have some kind of run-in with the police. For some people, interacting with the police can be a scary situation—especially if the run-in is not a friendly one. The good news is that you have rights when it comes to these interactions with the police. These rights keep the police from forcing you to say things you don't want to or from illegally getting evidence from you to then use against you.

Before we get into your rights, it would be helpful to explain where these rights came from. Since this isn't an American history textbook *and* we don't want to bore you, we'll give you a very short lesson on the origin of your rights when dealing with the police.

Back in the late 1700s, America consisted of a few colonies owned by the British Empire. The British king, George III, treated the American colonists very wrong by taxing them without any input from the colonists. King George also forced the colonists to put his soldiers up in their homes. Not only that, but if the British leaders and soldiers suspected any of the colonists of not supporting the king, they were allowed to barge into the colonists' homes and go through their papers and personal items to collect evidence to use against the suspected king haters.

All of this (and other) poor treatment by King George caused the American colonists to turn on him. The colonists were so sick and tired of King George that they decided to fight a war against Britain. That war, known as the Revolutionary War, ensued between the American colonies and Britain.

The colonies won. They were then free from British rule and decided to form a new independent country called the United States of America. The leaders of the colonies got together and drafted a document that spelled out how the country would be set up and run. They called this document the *Constitution*. The writers of the Constitution were called the *Founder*s and you've probably heard the names of some of these men—George Washington, Thomas Jefferson, Ben Franklin, and John Adams, just to name a few.

Although the Constitution covered a lot of information, a few things were missing—such as rules stating people's rights when encountering the authorities (such as the police). The Founders thought about how the British authorities could barge into people's homes without good reason or without permission. They also remembered how the British authorities could snatch citizens up and lock them up for no good reason.

To make the Constitution better, the Founders added more rules to it. These added rules are called *Amendments*. These Amendments included new rules that spelled out *rights* that citizens have when dealing with law enforcement. The specific Amendments that give you special rights when it comes to the police are the Fourth, Fifth, and Sixth Amendments. You can find the Constitution in any library, Social Studies textbook, or on the Internet. And that's the end of the history lesson.

Here's the basic rule about your rights and the police: if the police violate your rights in order to nab you for something, they're breaking the law. If you can point out the violation, you might be able to avoid being convicted if charged with a crime—this is why you need to know your rights.

The police can't just do whatever they want in order to lock you up. Because of the Constitution, the police have to follow rules to arrest you or to search you or your property. But you have to be on your toes and know your rights.

To Sum Up

The government (specifically, the police) has to follow certain rules in order to catch and punish citizens. You have rights that the police have to respect—rights given to you by the Constitution of the United States of America. If the police violate these rights, you might be able to avoid punishment.

CHAPTER RECAP

Concept Review of Chapter 11

- The rights that you have when dealing with the police are derived from the Constitution of the United States.

- The Constitution is a document that was drafted by the individuals who founded the United States of America. Among other things, it spells out the powers of the government and sets limits on the powers of law enforcement.

- The specific parts of the Constitution concerned with citizens' rights when dealing with law enforcement are the Fourth, Fifth, and Sixth Amendments.

- The police must follow rules in order to search and/or seize your things or you.

- If it can be shown that the police did not follow the rules in order to search and/or seize you or your things, you may be able to avoid government punishment.

THINK ABOUT IT
Reflection #11

Why is it important that people have rights? Have you or someone you know ever been in a situation where you believe rights were violated? Please explain your answer.

Chapter 12
Searches and Seizures

IMPORTANT WORDS
Search Warrant
Probable Cause
Seizure

This chapter focuses on the rules the police have to follow in order to search you and your property. It also discusses the rules the police have to follow to seize (snatch up) not only your possessions but YOU as well!

Can you think of why the police would want to search you and/or your property? The answer is that by searching you and/or your property, they may be able to find evidence that they can use to build a case against you. So, you should understand the importance of making sure that the police can't just barge into your house and have a look around whenever they please. As stated in Chapter 11, there are rules that law enforcement has to follow if and when they conduct searches of you or your possessions.

Privacy is the Key

In the United States of America, we expect privacy in certain places and situations. For instance, we expect privacy in our homes.

The government understands and respects the fact that citizens expect privacy in certain places and situations. As a result,

the government restricts itself from being able to invade a person's privacy in situations and places where the person has a legitimate expectation of privacy. Legitimate just means "real." In other words, in situations where you have a real expectation of privacy, the police have to get permission from you or a judge if they want to invade that privacy to conduct a search to find evidence to use against you.

How can you tell if you have a real expectation of privacy in a situation or place? To find out, two test questions have to be answered first. These are:

1. Do you expect some level of privacy in the situation or place?

2. Even if you do, would most other people think that you have a right to privacy in that place or situation?

Think about your house for a moment. You have a real expectation of privacy when you're in your home. We know this by asking and answering the two test questions:

1. Do you expect some level of privacy in your house? Yes, you expect some level of privacy in your home.

2. Would most other people think that you have an expectation of privacy in your house? Yes, most people would agree that you and all others have an expectation of privacy in their own homes.

So the answer is, yes, you do have a real expectation of privacy in your house.

What about a public park? Do you have a real expectation of privacy there? Let's find out by asking the two test questions:

1. Do you expect some level of privacy in a public park? No, it's open to the public so you should expect people to see and hear whatever you're doing while there.

2. Would most other people think that you have an expectation of privacy in the park? No, it's a public park and most people would agree that you do not have an expectation of privacy in a public park. If you're smooching with somebody in the park, you shouldn't be surprised when somebody shouts, "Get a room!" You can't honestly say that you really expected privacy in the park.

So the answer here is, no, you don't have a real expectation of privacy in a public park.

The house and public park examples were pretty easy. But there are some situations and places where it's hard to tell if you have an expectation of privacy. For instance, you might think that the police can't go through your garbage sitting at the curb without permission. Well, you'd be wrong. You don't have a real expectation of privacy in your trash once you've put it out to be collected. In other words, the police can search your trash placed on the curb without getting permission from you or a judge.

One of the best ways to tell if you have a real expectation of privacy besides asking the two test questions is to ask yourself if somebody could easily see or hear whatever it is you're trying to keep private. If so, you probably don't have a real expectation of privacy in that situation or place.

You might think that because you have an expectation of privacy in your home, the same applies to your backyard. This is partially true but not totally. While you might have a small expectation of privacy in your backyard, for the most part, you shouldn't. Since the police can fly over your property and scan it, or look through fence holes, or even climb on top of a nearby building to scope out your yard, you really don't have much of an expectation of privacy in your backyard. This is something to think about if you've ever contemplated growing illegal "plants" or hiding stolen merchandise in your backyard.

What about school? Do you have an expectation of privacy there? Not really. Although regular police officers are not allowed to search your things without probable cause (probable cause is discussed in the following paragraphs), school officials are allowed to search your bags, your locker, and even your car if it is on school property.

Search Warrants and Probable Cause

If the police want to invade your privacy and conduct a search of your property, they have to get a *search warrant*, which is basically a permission slip signed by a judge. Examples of search warrants can be found at the back of this book.

In order to get the search warrant, police officers have to show the judge they have *probable cause*—that is, something that the police can point to that would make the average cop, based on his or her experience as a cop, think that a crime was committed and that evidence of that crime will be found where the police want to search.

Think of probable cause as reasons the police have to give to the judge in order to get a warrant. But they're supposed to be good reasons. The cop can't just tell the judge, "Your honor, I can't really tell you why but I have a hunch something is up with this guy and I know we'll find drugs in his house if you give us a warrant." A hunch is not probable cause.

See pages 95–96 for an example of probable cause in action.

In the example, the police don't give Malcolm an apology. They don't help put his house back in order. They don't pay for the stuff they broke. Worst of all, Malcolm can't sue them or do anything because their search was legal. They had probable cause and got a search warrant. See, any average cop with experience on the force would have thought that Malcolm committed the crime and that evidence of the crime would be found at Malcolm's house based on the description given by the cashier.

Seizures

Usually the word *seizure* makes people think of a person convulsing uncontrollably. In the legal sense, it has a different meaning. Seizure applies to the police taking your possessions or taking you; so when the cops snatch you up, they are seizing you. And if they take your stuff, they've seized your stuff.

In the previous example, where Officers Petti and Grimes searched Malcolm's house for evidence of the gas station robbery, if they had found some cash and a Snickers candy bar in a drawer, a shotgun hanging on Malcolm's bedroom wall, and four packs of Kools cigarettes sitting on the kitchen counter, they could take all of that from Malcolm's house as evidence of the robbery. In other words, they could "seize" all of those items.

Luckily, the police have to play by certain rules before they can snatch up (seize) you or your possessions. If the items or person they want to seize is not out in public, they have to get a search warrant to look for what they want to find. The search warrant has to say what places they can search and what people and things they can search for.

Even though the police are limited to searching only for the people listed on a warrant, if they reasonably suspect that people hanging out at your house might have weapons on them, they're allowed to pat those people down for weapons—even if their names aren't on the warrant.

Here's an example of this type of situation:

Malcolm goes over to Carlos's house to hang out. All of sudden, a S.W.A.T. team busts in through Carlos's front door and they have a warrant! It's a drug raid, and the police think Carlos is a drug dealer. Because most drug dealers have weapons to protect themselves from being shot, the police pat Carlos down to make sure he doesn't have a gun. They also figure that any dude who hangs around a dealer is probably holding a weapon, too. So they pat Malcolm down, too, even though his name isn't on the warrant.

Now that you have some knowledge about searches and seizures, the next thing you should be concerned about is how do you protect yourself when the cops come knockin' at your door.

To Sum Up

You have an expectation of privacy in certain places and situations. The police have to respect this expectation of privacy. If the police violate your privacy in order to get evidence to use against you or to take your stuff or even you, they are breaking the law.

CHAPTER RECAP
Concept Review of Chapter 12

- In situations where you have a legitimate expectation of privacy, the police must get permission from either you or a judge in order to invade that privacy and conduct a search.

- You have a legitimate expectation of privacy in any situation or place where:

- You reasonably expect some level of privacy, AND

- The situation or place is one where society in general would also agree that privacy should be expected.

- School officials are not restricted by the same laws as police officers when it comes to searching your things on school property.

- A search warrant is a document signed by a judge that allows the police to invade your privacy to search for evidence against you.

- The police must have probable cause to get a search warrant.

- Probable cause is anything that an average cop—based on his or her experience as a cop—could use to justify a belief that a crime was committed, that a particular person committed the crime, and that evidence of that crime will be found in a specific place.

- When the police take your stuff during a search, it is called a seizure.

- The police must have probable cause to seize your things.

  The police can only search and seize things that are listed on their search warrant.

THINK ABOUT IT
Reflection #12

What rules do the police have to follow in searching and seizing you and your property? How can you protect yourself from unlawful search and seizure?

Chapter 13

What to Do When the Cops Come Knockin'

If the police do come knocking at your door, you have two immediate options. You can ignore them or you can answer the door. Now, if they have an arrest warrant (not a search warrant) and reasonably think you're hiding inside, they might end up busting the door down anyway. If you decide to answer the door and the officers say they have an arrest warrant, you should go outside to talk to them. Make sure to shut the door behind you when you do.

On the other hand, if the police don't say they have a warrant for your arrest, don't step outside. Talk to them from inside the house, preferably with the door slightly open. This book will explain in greater detail what to do if the cops come knocking with an arrest warrant. For now, this chapter will concentrate on what to do when the police come knocking with a search warrant in hand.

What to Do if the Police Have a Search Warrant

If the police ask to come in, calmly ask them from behind your closed door if they have a search warrant. If they do, open the door and read it to make sure that it's legitimate.

Make sure that the warrant has your correct address. A warrant is not legitimate if the address is wrong—even if just one number is off. If you live in an apartment or condo, it should have your apartment number and not just the building number.

Make sure that the date on the warrant is fairly recent. If the date is more than a couple of weeks old, it may not be valid.

Finally, make sure that the warrant has a judge's signature on it. If there's no signature where the judge or magistrate (a type of judge) is supposed to sign, the warrant is useless.

An illegitimate warrant means the police aren't allowed to come in. But, you have to tell them that you don't consent to them searching your house or your possessions because the warrant isn't right. How do you do that? Just tell them what's wrong with the warrant and then say, "I don't consent to you searching my home or my stuff." See the example on page 100.

What if the police ignore you and decide to go in and search your house and your possessions anyway? Should you physically try to stop them? The answer should

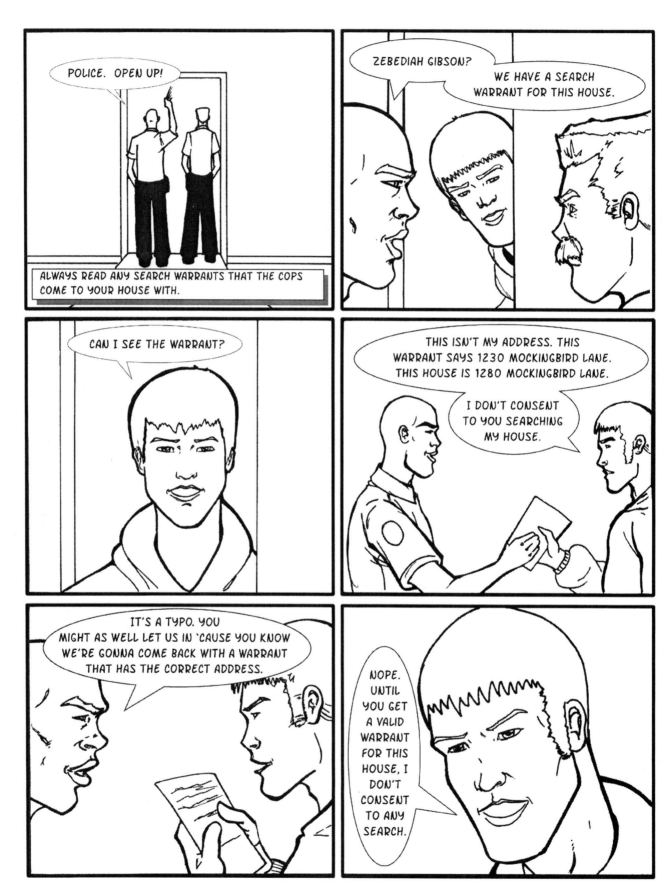

be obvious—NO! Never physically try to stop the police from going into your house. If you do choose to try to physically stop the cops from entering your home, one of three things will more than likely happen:

- They'll decide not to go in after all and do nothing to you (highly unlikely).

- They'll beat you so horribly that you'll think twice about ever putting your hands on a cop again—and they'll still go in.

- They'll kill you—and they'll still end up going in.

Which of the above scenarios do you think is most likely to happen? If you value your health and your life, be smart and let them be. Just make sure to file a report and to tell your attorney that the police ignored you when you told them that their warrant wasn't valid and that you did not consent to them going into your house and/or searching your possessions.

The Police Trashing Your House During a Search

When the police search your stuff, don't expect them to handle your things with love—it's likely they're going to trash your place. If they do, they're not going to clean the mess up, either. What should you do? Take pictures of your place after the police have trashed it and give them to your attorney.

Giving the Police Permission to Search Your Home and Possessions

The easiest way for a cop to get in and search your house, your stuff, or even you is by getting *your* permission. This is how some cops avoid the hassle of having to convince a judge to give them a warrant. No warrant is required if you give them permission to invade your privacy.

Because the police know that they can search people's property without a warrant if you give them the okay, they sometimes try to trick people into giving them permission to conduct a search of their property. For instance, an officer might walk up to you on the street and act real friendly, asking to check out your duffle bag. She'll say something like, "Hey, mind if I take a look in your bag?" Or she may reach for your bag and simply say, "You don't mind, do you?" Without thinking, and probably because you're a little intimidated, you tell her okay. Before you know it, she's going through your bag.

If a cop walks up to you on the street and asks to have a look at your personal items, such as a bag, purse, or backpack, simply say, "Officer, I don't consent to you searching my things." Then try to keep moving along.

If the police come to your house and want to search it but don't have a warrant, you can refuse. You can do this by saying, "Officer, I do not give you permission to search my house or my things." Yes, you'll sound stiff and somewhat corny, but say it like this anyway. When you use slang or street language, the police can claim that they didn't understand that you were telling them they weren't allowed to search your house. Keep the conversation short and sweet so that you don't end up saying anything that makes you look or sound guilty.

Though most police officers are honest and would never plant evidence, you never know when you may encounter a dishonest

cop. This is why it's hardly ever a good idea to give the police permission to search your house or your possessions if they don't have a warrant.

You should know that it doesn't matter how menacing they try to act, if the police don't have a warrant, they have to get your permission to search your house and/or your possessions. The only exceptions are when somebody inside is in danger, when they are chasing a suspect and he or she runs into your house, or when they reasonably think somebody inside is trying to get rid of evidence (such as flushing dope down the toilet).

The cops are not supposed to intimidate or force you into giving them permission to search your property. Your permission always has to be voluntary—meaning you gave it because you wanted to. Permission isn't voluntary if the police trick you into letting them in by lying about having a warrant, flashing their weapons, or nagging and nagging you for permission after you've told them no.

Avoiding a Police Search When Throwing a Party

Who doesn't like a good party? It's fun to be able to cut loose and party sometimes. But if you're the person throwing the party, you'd better maintain control over the situation. Make it clear to your party guests that they cannot bring weapons, drugs, or any other illegal stuff to your party. Leave the guy who's always starting some drama off the invite list.

Telling your friends to keep your front and back doors closed and locked during the party is key. If you don't, the cops can come in without a warrant and without asking permission—just like anybody else coming to the party. Be sure to check around the house to make sure that your guests are not participating in any illegal activities such as smoking illegal substances. Remember, when something goes down at *your* house, you're the one on the line.

If the cops show up at your party and the smell of illegal substances is floating in the air, they won't be listening to you telling them you didn't know people were upstairs smoking or that any drugs they find at the party aren't yours. *Your* house means *your* drugs—even if they really aren't. This is why it's extremely important to make sure that any party you throw is totally under control.

To Sum Up

When the police come to your home and want to come in, always ask for a search warrant. Read the warrant and make sure that it is valid. If the warrant isn't valid, make the police aware of this and tell them that you don't consent to a search. If they try to go in anyway, do not try to physically stop them.

It's usually not a good idea to give the cops permission to search your things if they ask. Politely tell them that you do not consent to a search if they ask to have a look inside your bags or pockets.

Be ultra careful when throwing a party. Remember that you could be held responsible for any illegal activity that goes on at your party, whether you are taking part in it or not.

CHAPTER RECAP

Concept Review of Chapter 13

- If the police come to your home with a search warrant (but not an arrest warrant), be sure to read the warrant carefully and make sure that all of the information on the warrant is correct.

- If some or all of the information on the search warrant is not correct (wrong name of the suspect, or wrong address, or is not signed by a judge or magistrate), you should tell the police that you do not consent to a search.

- Never physically try to stop the police from entering your home. Instead, tell your attorney that the police entered even after you verbally denied them permission.

- If the police trash your home during a search, take pictures of the damage and give them to your attorney.

- If a cop stops you on the street and asks to search your personal items such as a backpack or purse, simply tell them that you do not consent to them searching your things.

- If the police come to your home without a search warrant, but ask to search your home anyway, it is usually not a good idea to give them permission to enter.

- Any permission that you give to the police to search you or your things must be voluntary. The police are not supposed to intimidate or force you into giving your consent.

- When throwing a party, you can be held responsible for anything brought in and out of the party, including drugs, weapons, and other illegal items.

- When throwing a party, it's best to keep your doors closed and locked.

THINK ABOUT IT
Reflection #13

How should you behave when you have an encounter with the police? Can you think of a time when you or someone you know responded incorrectly to a police encounter? Please explain. What do you think they should have done differently?

Chapter 14

Cars Are the Danger Zone

The Danger Zone

If you're of driving age or soon will be, you should read this chapter very carefully. Cars are the *danger zone* when it comes to police searches. The first thing to know about police searching cars is that it's really easy for the police to get the right to search your car without a warrant. There are a few reasons why. First off, unlike most houses, cars move. This means any evidence that's inside a car can be driven away. Second, you don't have much of an expectation of privacy in your car. Why not? Well, think about it: anybody can see inside most people's cars easily. And even though some cars have heavily tinted windows, most have clear ones.

Since cars are mobile, and because you don't have much of an expectation of privacy in your car, the cops can search it without jumping through the hoops they have to in order to search your house. This doesn't mean the police can search your car when and wherever they want. They still have to have probable cause. They just don't have to get a warrant once they have it. In other words, they can search your car right on the spot.

The cops can pull you over for some legitimate reason such as failure to stop at a red light or some other traffic violation. If, after they've pulled you over, they notice you trying to slide a plastic bag with what looks like "herbs" under your passenger seat, they've got probable cause to search your car. See, it looks like you're trying to hide an illegal substance. Most cops, based on their experience with fighting crime, would think you had drugs on you. It should go without saying that you should be very careful about who you let ride with you. If you have friends who tend to have drugs on them, giving them a ride is not the smartest thing to do.

What to Do When You Get Pulled Over

Whenever the police pull you over, act natural, stay relaxed, and wait for the officer to approach the car. Never get out of your car unless the officer tells you to. Keep your hands where the officer can see them—on the steering wheel is fine but keep your grip on the wheel loose. A tight grip on the steering wheel can make cops nervous.

Roll down your window and speak as pleasantly as you can to the officer. Be sure to look straight at him or her when you speak. Always have your registration and insurance in a place where you don't have to fumble around to get them. If your papers are in your glove box, calmly tell the officer that your papers are in there, and ask if it's okay to reach inside and get them. Get them out only after the officer approves it. Do all of this as calmly as possible. You don't want to make a cop jumpy.

If the cop starts asking questions, keep it simple. You can tell the police who you are, where you live, and where you're going. Other than that, you shouldn't answer any other questions. Definitely don't answer if asked if you know why you were stopped. Instead, ask if he or she would like your license and registration. If the officer keeps asking questions instead of taking your license and registration, respectfully say that you're going to decline answering any questions and that you're going to remain silent until you speak to an attorney.

Usually, the officer will take your license and papers, run a check on you, and decide whether to write you a ticket. When he or she gives your license and papers back (along, most likely, with a ticket), you should be able to ride out.

Above all, be polite and respectful during the whole situation. Do not yell at cops about what they can and can't do to you and how you know your rights and such. This is a sure way to get a nightstick crack upside your forehead.

If the cop asks to search your car, say that you do not give permission to do so. Then ask if you're free to leave. If he or she says yes, go ahead and ride out. If the cop says no, you're under arrest, and you need to tell the officer that you're going to remain silent and that you want to speak to an attorney. Then don't say anything else—period.

If the cop doesn't say anything when you ask if you're free to leave, tell the officer that you assume you can leave because of his silence, and attempt to drive off safely. If the cop prevents you from leaving, you're under arrest, and you need to tell the officer that you're not saying anything and that you'd like an attorney.

To Sum Up

Your car is the danger zone because you don't have much of an expectation of privacy when you're in it. This means that the cops don't have to follow as many rules in order to search it as they would for something like your house. Never drive with anything that you wouldn't want the police discovering. And if you're ever pulled over, stay calm and don't say too much.

CHAPTER RECAP

Concept Review of Chapter 14

- Whenever you are driving, always have your license, registration, and insurance in a place where you can easily reach them without fumbling for them.

- If you are ever pulled over by the police, be cool, calm, and polite.

- If the police ask for permission to search your car, do not give it to them.

- Sometimes an officer will take your license, insurance, and registration to run a check on you and/or to write you a ticket. When he or she returns these things to you (along, most likely, with a ticket), ask if you are free to leave. If the officer says no, ask for a lawyer and don't say anything else.

THINK ABOUT IT
Reflection #14

Have you or someone you know ever been pulled over by the police while driving? If so, what happened during the stop? What steps can be taken to avoid having your rights violated by police during a traffic stop?

Chapter 15
Arrests

What Is an Arrest?

This chapter will discuss the basic rules law enforcement officers have to follow when it comes to seizing (snatching up) *you*. We're talking about *arrests*. Knowing when you're under arrest is key because you have certain rights that kick in when you're under arrest.

Believe it or not, it's not always easy to know when you're under arrest. Most people think that you're only under arrest when the cops *tell* you that you're under arrest, when they start reading you your rights, or when they put their hands on you to keep you from going anywhere.

It's true that you *are* under arrest in all of the above situations. But did you know that you can be under arrest regardless of whether the cops tell you that you are, whether they read you your rights, and whether they put their hands on you or not?

Whenever you are not free to leave when the police are questioning you somewhere, you are under arrest. Now don't misunderstand, the cops can *detain* you to ask you questions. A police detention is not an arrest because you can leave if you want. In other words, the police can stop you on the street to ask you questions and they can even take you down to the station to ask you questions—if you agree to go with them.

You're not under arrest just because the police stop you and ask you questions or because they take you to the station to question you (if you agree to go with them). You are only under arrest when you can't leave if you want to.

Because the police are unlikely to inform you when they are detaining you that you can leave if you want, it's hard to tell if you're under arrest. So what do you do?

The answer is simple: you *ask* the police if you're free leave. It's that simple. Ideally, when you ask, the police will answer with a simple yes or no. If they say yes, don't answer any more questions and move along. If they say no, you're under arrest even if they haven't told you that you are. The best thing that you can do at this point is to keep your mouth shut—when you're under arrest, you have the right to remain silent. Use it. The next few sections in this chapter discuss your rights when under arrest.

Sometimes, the cops will give you a direct answer when you ask if you're free to leave. Sometimes, they won't. Instead, they might try to dodge answering. If they do this, just say, "Officer, since you haven't told me that I have to stay here and answer your questions, I'm going to go ahead and leave, unless you're ordering me to stay." After you've told them you're leaving, LEAVE! If they won't let you leave by putting their hands on you, or they block or start crowding you as you're trying to walk away, you're under arrest.

If you're wondering if the cops are supposed to read you your rights when they arrest you, the answer is no. They're only required to read your rights to you when they're arresting you AND questioning you. In other words, if they're just arresting you but not asking you questions, they don't have to read you your rights. Or if they are questioning you but aren't arresting you, they don't have to read you your rights. This is why it's important to know when you're under arrest.

If the police are arresting you and asking you questions but fail to read you your rights, this doesn't mean that they're not allowed to take you in. It just means that whatever you tell them can't be used against you if you end up going to trial.

Your Rights During an Arrest

When you're arrested, you have two very important rights. The first has been mentioned previously—the right to remain silent. The second right is the right to an attorney whenever the cops ask you questions. These are important rights because they could be the difference between doing jail time and walking free.

Your Right to Remain Silent

Most folks are their own worst enemies when dealing with the cops. Never mind snitches or evidence—your mouth is the thing most likely to hurt you. Remember, anything you say when you talk to the police, whether or not you're under arrest, can be used against you later in court.

You have to use some judgment when the police are asking you questions. They may or may not be questioning you because they suspect that you did something wrong. Maybe they're only questioning you as a witness. It's up to you to decide if you should talk or not. If something doesn't feel right about their questions, though, you need to keep your mouth shut. Again, you do this by telling the cops respectfully that you're going to decline answering their questions. Find out if you're free to leave. If you're not, tell the police that you're going to remain silent and that you want to speak to an attorney.

Speaking of attorneys, if you can't afford one, the government must give you one. You may not be able to see your court-appointed attorney right away, though. You may have to sit in a cell for a while, possibly days. Still, do not talk to the police, prosecutors, judges, guards, or any other government person until you've talked to your attorney. It's not a good idea to talk to other offenders around you either because they might tell the police what you've said.

Here are some other rules about arrests:

1. The police must have probable cause to arrest you—meaning they have to believe reasonably that you committed a crime or are about to commit a crime to arrest you.

2. The police can arrest you in a public place without an arrest warrant.

3. The police usually need an arrest warrant to come into your house and arrest you.

What to Do When the Police Want to Arrest You at Your House

As stated above, the police usually need an arrest warrant to come into your house and arrest you. Of course, if the police only have a search warrant, they can come into your house, find some incriminating evidence, and *then* arrest you without an arrest warrant.

The police don't need an arrest warrant to arrest you in public. But did you know that a porch is considered public? That's right—if you're on your porch, the police don't need an arrest warrant to snatch you off of it. This is why you need to be *inside* your house when the cops come knockin'. And if the police don't have an arrest warrant, do not step outside.

What if the cops show up with an arrest warrant? The best thing to do is to open your door slightly, slide through, and step outside to read the warrant. If you open your door wide, the police might hear or see something that gives them the right to go in without a search warrant. Confirm that the warrant has your name on it, that it has a judge's or magistrate's signature, and that the date is recent. If the warrant is correct, go with the police immediately. Of course, if it is not correct, you can alert the police to this fact, but it is not a good idea to resist arrest if they insist on taking you in. Just be sure to tell your attorney that the arrest warrant was incorrect. An example

of an arrest warrant is shown at the back of this book. Depending on where you live, an arrest warrant may look different from the example but all arrest warrants should meet the basic requirements of having the correct person(s) named on it, a judge or magistrate's signature, and is recent.

It's usually not a good idea to go back into the house to get anything. This is because, once the cops arrest you, they can't let you out of their sight. So if they let you go back into the house, they're allowed to follow you in. Once inside, they might find some evidence that makes you look guilty.

If the police have an arrest warrant and you didn't come out and immediately go with them, they can go into your house to get you. They can also pat you down and search anywhere your arms can reach. So if your arms can reach near a closet, they can search the closet. They're allowed to do this to protect themselves from you being able to reach out and grab something to hurt them with. They're not supposed to be looking for stuff other than weapons that you could reach for (unless they also have search warrant for other items). But if they think that somebody who might hurt or kill them is hiding in the house, they can search wherever they think the person might be hiding—which means they can pretty much search the whole house.

To Sum Up

When you are placed under arrest, you have certain rights. If you're not sure that you're under arrest, ask if you are. If it turns out that you're under arrest, tell the police that you're going to remain silent and would like to speak to an attorney. After you've done that, keep your mouth shut.

CHAPTER RECAP
Concept Review of Chapter 15

- An arrest is a police seizure of you.

- You are not necessarily under arrest because you are being detained by the police. You are under arrest when you are not free to leave.

- The best way to know if you are free to leave when the police detain you is by asking them.

- When you are under arrest, you have the right to remain silent and to have an attorney present while being questioned.

- Remember that your right to remain silent when arrested is very important. Anything that you say that sounds incriminating will likely be used against you in court.

- The police do not need a warrant to arrest you in public. All that they need is probable cause.

- The police usually need to have a warrant to arrest you at your home if you are inside the home. If, however, you are outside the house (on your porch, for instance), all the police need is probable cause and they are not required to get a warrant.

- If the police come to your home with a legitimate arrest warrant, it is usually best not to go back into the house to get anything. This is because the police are allowed to follow you back inside. They then have the right to search anywhere your arms can reach. If they reasonably suspect someone dangerous is hiding in the home, they can search wherever they reasonably think the person may be hiding.

THINK ABOUT IT
Reflection #15

What would you do if you were being arrested? How would you behave and what would you tell the police? Please write out what you would do step by step.

Chapter 16

The Police Own the Streets

IMPORTANT WORDS
Reasonable Suspicion
Frisk
Drug Courier Profile
Racial and Ethnic Profiling

Your home might be your castle, but the streets belong to the police. The police can stop you briefly for a pat down in public any time they have a reasonable suspicion that you might be involved in, or are about to commit, a crime.

Reasonable suspicion sounds a lot like probable cause, but they are not exactly the same thing. Like probable cause, *reasonable suspicion* is basically a good reason or multiple reasons why the cop thinks something is going down. So how is reasonable suspicion different from probable cause? Well, with reasonable suspicion, the reasons don't have to be as "good" as they have to be for probable cause.

With reasonable suspicion, the officer only needs to have a very tiny reason to stop, question, or frisk you. The law allows cops to use the experience gained as police officers in determining if they have reasonable suspicion. For example, if a cop sees a person hanging out on the corner, walking up and "shaking hands" with people who drive up in cars, and then going back to stand on the corner, the cop might, based on his or her experience, have a reasonable suspicion that the person is dealing drugs. So he or she is allowed to question and to frisk the person.

Police Frisks

The police can stop and *frisk* you (pat you down in search of weapons or illegal items) if they have good reason to believe that you're holding a weapon on you. And if, while frisking you for a weapon, cops feel something that seems to be some illegal stuff (such as drugs), they can go all through your pockets.

Dressing and Acting Like a Thug

Fair or not, you take a risk when you try to imitate the dress and behavior of drug dealers, "gangstas," and even rappers. Imitating these folks is a sure-fire way to bring attention from the cops.

The government allows the cops to mess with you based on how you dress and act even if they don't directly see you doing anything illegal. Dress and/or act like a drug dealer and the cops will hassle you like one; you see, cops pretty much get a free pass to hassle anyone who fits a drug-courier profile.

The *drug-courier profile* is the set of behaviors that people who traffic drugs exhibit. In other words, drug traffickers tend to do certain things and act a certain way. If you do those things or act in that way, the cops can bother you. If you want to know if you fit a drug-courier profile, ask yourself the following questions:

- Do you wear the types of clothes that a drug dealer usually wears (white T-shirts, certain types of sneakers, hoodies, etc.)?

- Do you wear your clothes the *way* drug dealers wear theirs (baggy jeans sagging way down your waist, extra-extra-long white T-shirts, baseball caps pointed to the side of town you represent, etc.)?

- Do you hang out with drug dealers?

- Do you go to the *places* drug dealers usually go (drug houses, strip clubs, or the drug corner)?

- Do you drive the types of *vehicles* drug dealers use to get around (black SUVs, especially with 22-inch rims or larger, or vehicles with heavily tinted windows)?

- Do you hang out with the *people* drug dealers associate with (drug users, high-school dropouts, convicted felons, etc.)?

- Do you have stuff that you can't possibly afford (an $80,000 car but you don't have a job)?

- Do you exhibit unexplainable or odd behaviors (you make many very short phone calls to the same phone numbers or you pay for everything in cash)?

Running When You See the Cops Coming Your Way

Did you know that if you're in a so-called "high-crime" area, the cops can stop and pat you down if you run when you see them coming your way? Running when you see the cops approaching basically gives them reasonable suspicion to stop and frisk you. Never mind that they may not really have a concrete reason to think that you've done anything.

You might think that it would be a good idea to go hang out in a nearby lower-crime neighborhood—that way you're less likely to get hassled by the cops, right? Maybe, but if you're a member of a race or ethnic group that isn't usually found in that neighborhood, the cops are allowed to hassle you. Regardless of whether it is fair or not, the cops are allowed to stop and pat you down on the street if you run when you see them approaching or you're a member of a racial or ethnic group that isn't ordinarily found in a certain area.

Staying Alive When Dealing with the Police

Being a police officer is a dangerous job. At any given time, police officers can walk into situations in which they can be seriously hurt or lose their lives. Because of the high possibility of running into violence, police officers themselves have to be ready to use force when dealing with crime.

When it comes to the use of deadly force to make an arrest, the police are only supposed to use it in special situations. They are only supposed to use deadly force if they have good reason to believe that the person they're arresting might seriously hurt or kill other people or to keep the arrested person from escaping. Most times, if possible, the cops are supposed to give a warning before they shoot to kill.

It is a reality that, while most cops use deadly force only as a last resort, some use it whenever they feel they can get away with it. Some use it because the dangerousness of a situation makes them jumpy and more likely to pull the trigger. When dealing with cops, you have to do your part to stay alive.

Any and all movements, sudden or not, can give a cop reason to use deadly force. If you find yourself being arrested, stay calm and relaxed. Only make movements the cop tells you to make. Talk calmly and respectfully to the cops and keep your hands where they can see them. Be extremely polite. The last thing you want to do is to give a cop with a short fuse or one who's extremely nervous a so-called "justified" reason to use deadly force on you. Keep calm and cool and you'll have a better chance of keeping your life.

Racial And Ethnic Profiling

Did you know that racial profiling is technically legal? The government doesn't really care if a police officer only chooses to arrest minorities—as long as he or she has probable cause to arrest them. This means that you could have a cop who, in twenty years on the force, has arrested 5,000 minorities and no non-minorities. This is allowed as long as the minorities arrested gave the officer probable cause to go after them. Basically, cops don't have to play fair when it comes to choosing whom to arrest.

Because racial and ethnic profiling is technically legal, it is important to avoid giving a biased cop probable cause to hassle you. The best advice is to obey the law. This doesn't guarantee that a bigoted cop won't hassle you, but it may cut down on the chances. Here are few quick tips to help you avoid becoming a victim of racial or ethnic profiling when driving.

- Obey the speed limit and all traffic laws.

- Make sure that all your exterior lights are working correctly.

- Make sure that you don't have stuff blocking your back window; in fact, make sure that none of your windows are tinted too darkly.

- Make certain that your license plate can be seen.

- Keep your car neat and clean on the inside and out.

- Be careful about "tricking out" your car. Check to see what your local and state rules are regarding modifying your car.

- Keep everything that's supposed to be inside the car, inside the car (feet, arms, smoke, trash, music)—driving around with your music blaring or any type of smoke puffing out of your car is an invitation for the cops to come and hassle you.

To Sum Up

Always be mindful that the way you dress and behave can bring unwanted police attention—so it's usually smart to minimize doing things that the police associate with criminal or thug-type people. It's important to keep your cool and to be relaxed and respectful when encountering the police.

CHAPTER RECAP
Concept Review of Chapter 16

- The police are allowed to frisk you if you are out in public and they have a reasonable suspicion that you have a weapon on you.

- Reasonable suspicion is less than probable cause, but has to be more than just a hunch. The law allows police officers to rely on their experience doing their job to determine if their suspicion is reasonable.

- The way you dress and act can activate a police officer's reasonable suspicion.

- The places you go and the people who you associate with can cause a cop to reasonably suspect that you are up to something unlawful.

- If you are in a "high-crime" area and start running when you see the police approaching, they are allowed to stop and frisk you. This is because your running gives them reasonable suspicion to think that you may have done, or are doing, something unlawful.

- Always be calm and respectful when encountering the police. Never make sudden moves and always keep your hands where they can see them.

- A biased or racist officer is technically allowed to practice discrimination and only arrest certain people if he or she has actual probable cause to arrest them.

- You should avoid doing things that would give a police officer probable cause to hassle you.

THINK ABOUT IT
Reflection #16

What would you do if you were walking down the street and the police stopped you to ask you some questions? How would you behave and what would you say to the police? Please write out what you would do step by step.

Conclusion:
The Power Is Yours, Now Use It

If you've thoroughly read *When the Cops Come Knockin'*, you should have learned some valuable information about criminal law and criminal procedure. You should have learned what it takes to be branded a criminal; the definitions of certain crimes; how easy it is to get involved in criminal activity; how to recognize, avoid, and remove yourself from criminal activity; what your rights are when dealing with law enforcement; and how to assert those rights. Because of the knowledge you've gained, you've also gained power—the power to save yourself from the criminal justice system.

Your newfound power is only going to be useful to you if you use it wisely. Although you may have learned a few things to keep the government from illegally searching and arresting you, the best thing you can do to stay out of trouble is to obey the laws in the first place. Once you're *in* the system, your fate is always going to be up in the air, no matter how much you know about the law.

For those who think they're too smart to ever get caught doing criminal activity,

think again. You *will* get caught, no matter how clever or "gangsta" you think you are. There's no way around it. It's like how you can go for a long time without catching a cold or the flu, but eventually, you will get sick because you can't avoid catching a cold forever. The justice system's job is to catch people who break the law or who cause results the government does not like to see. You may be able to outsmart these people for a while, but if you keep going, they *will* eventually catch you. And when they do, they will make you pay a price. Bottom line: try to avoid criminal activities and associating with people who are involved in criminal activity.

From this book, you've also learned that there are rules law enforcement has to follow whenever they want to search or arrest you. If you can show that they didn't follow those rules, you may be able to save yourself from government punishment.

The Constitution doesn't allow the government to use any evidence at your trial against you obtained by violating the rules. But you (or preferably, your lawyer) have to point out the violations. This is why it's a good idea to keep track of everything that happens whenever you encounter law enforcement. It all comes down to you being smart enough to catch when law enforcement doesn't follow the rules. Here are some tips for keeping track of whether they're following the rules—some of which you've already read about in this book:

- Find out if the police or other law enforcement personnel have a legitimate warrant to search or arrest you—read the warrant closely!

- Pay attention to how rough the cops are with you when trying to search or arrest you.

- Note whether the cops just busted into your spot to do the search without any warning, or if they knocked, yelled out "police," and asked to come in to do the search.

- Whenever you're being searched or stopped without a warrant, keep track of how long they keep you from leaving.

- Whenever a search or arrest is over, as soon as you find yourself with free time, write down exactly what happened, how it happened, when it happened, who was there, and what was said.

Using these tips will keep you from forgetting important facts that could be helpful later when you try to get evidence thrown out in court.

Life is about choices and the consequences of those choices. With the knowledge you've gained from reading *When the Cops Come Knockin'*, you should now be well equipped to make choices that will keep you out of the clutches of the criminal justice system.

The End
Post-Assessment

Directions

Now that you have finished the book, please take a few moments to answer the following questions to see how much you have learned from reading this book. Please check the number of the answer that represents your awareness of criminal law, the legal system, and how to protect your rights.

GENERAL AWARENESS OF THE LAW

ANSWER	RATING
Strongly Agree	5
Agree	4
Uncertain	3
Disagree	2
Strongly Disagree	1

1. I have a clear understanding of criminal law, the legal system, and how to protect my legal rights.

   ☐ 5 ☐ 4 ☐ 3 ☐ 2 ☐ 1

2. I have a clear understanding of what a crime is.

   ☐ 5 ☐ 4 ☐ 3 ☐ 2 ☐ 1

3. I have a clear understanding of what makes a person a criminal.

   ☐ 5 ☐ 4 ☐ 3 ☐ 2 ☐ 1

4. I have a clear understanding of what laws are.

   ☐ 5 ☐ 4 ☐ 3 ☐ 2 ☐ 1

5. I have a clear understanding of why laws are important.

   ☐ 5 ☐ 4 ☐ 3 ☐ 2 ☐ 1

6. I can explain the concept of willful blindness.

   ☐ 5 ☐ 4 ☐ 3 ☐ 2 ☐ 1

7. I have a clear understanding of what criminal negligence is.

   ☐ 5 ☐ 4 ☐ 3 ☐ 2 ☐ 1

8. I have a clear understanding of what criminal recklessness is.

   ☐ 5 ☐ 4 ☐ 3 ☐ 2 ☐ 1

9. I can explain how not thinking and caring about my actions can lead to my being punished for a crime.

   ☐ 5 ☐ 4 ☐ 3 ☐ 2 ☐ 1

10. I can define the crime of larceny.

    ☐ 5 ☐ 4 ☐ 3 ☐ 2 ☐ 1

11. I can recognize the difference between the crimes of burglary and robbery.

    ☐ 5 ☐ 4 ☐ 3 ☐ 2 ☐ 1

12. I know what bullying is and its consequences.

    ☐ 5 ☐ 4 ☐ 3 ☐ 2 ☐ 1

13. I know how to fight against bullying.

    ☐ 5 ☐ 4 ☐ 3 ☐ 2 ☐ 1

14. I can describe different situations in which a person could be charged with murder.

    ☐ 5 ☐ 4 ☐ 3 ☐ 2 ☐ 1

15. I can distinguish between murder and involuntary manslaughter.

    ☐ 5 ☐ 4 ☐ 3 ☐ 2 ☐ 1

16. I understand what an inchoate crime is and can name several.

    ☐ 5 ☐ 4 ☐ 3 ☐ 2 ☐ 1

17. I can define the crime of conspiracy.

    ☐ 5 ☐ 4 ☐ 3 ☐ 2 ☐ 1

18. I can describe what an accomplice to a crime is.

    ☐ 5 ☐ 4 ☐ 3 ☐ 2 ☐ 1

19. I understand what a strict liability crime is.

    ☐ 5 ☐ 4 ☐ 3 ☐ 2 ☐ 1

20. I can explain the difference between statutory rape and rape.

    ☐ 5 ☐ 4 ☐ 3 ☐ 2 ☐ 1

21. I can recognize situations and circumstances that might lead to my involvement in criminal behavior.

    ☐ 5 ☐ 4 ☐ 3 ☐ 2 ☐ 1

22. I have a good understanding of my rights regarding searches and seizures.

    ☐ 5 ☐ 4 ☐ 3 ☐ 2 ☐ 1

23. I understand the dangers of "sexting" and cyberbullying.

  ☐ 5 ☐ 4 ☐ 3 ☐ 2 ☐ 1

24. I understand the dangers of playing with fire.

  ☐ 5 ☐ 4 ☐ 3 ☐ 2 ☐ 1

25. I understand the consequences of underage drinking.

  ☐ 5 ☐ 4 ☐ 3 ☐ 2 ☐ 1

26. I understand what disorderly conduct and obstruction of justice are.

  ☐ 5 ☐ 4 ☐ 3 ☐ 2 ☐ 1

27. I understand what legal defenses are and can name a few.

  ☐ 5 ☐ 4 ☐ 3 ☐ 2 ☐ 1

28. I have a clear understanding of what constitutes self-defense and what does not.

  ☐ 5 ☐ 4 ☐ 3 ☐ 2 ☐ 1

29. I know what unlawful force is.

  ☐ 5 ☐ 4 ☐ 3 ☐ 2 ☐ 1

30. I understand the rules for defending my property.

  ☐ 5 ☐ 4 ☐ 3 ☐ 2 ☐ 1

31. I understand when the law requires a duty to help a person in danger.

  ☐ 5 ☐ 4 ☐ 3 ☐ 2 ☐ 1

32. I understand what to do if I have contact with the police.

  ☐ 5 ☐ 4 ☐ 3 ☐ 2 ☐ 1

33. I have a clear understanding of what probable cause is.

  ☐ 5 ☐ 4 ☐ 3 ☐ 2 ☐ 1

34. I can describe the difference between probable cause and reasonable suspicion.

  ☐ 5 ☐ 4 ☐ 3 ☐ 2 ☐ 1

35. I can explain what a search warrant is and what to look for when reading one.

  ☐ 5 ☐ 4 ☐ 3 ☐ 2 ☐ 1

36. I understand the difference between a search warrant and an arrest warrant.

  ☐ 5 ☐ 4 ☐ 3 ☐ 2 ☐ 1

37. I have a clear understanding of what an arrest is.

  ☐ 5 ☐ 4 ☐ 3 ☐ 2 ☐ 1

38. I can explain the importance of the Constitution of the United States as it applies to my rights when dealing with law enforcement.

☐ 5 ☐ 4 ☐ 3 ☐ 2 ☐ 1

39. I understand the concept of "expectation of privacy" as it applies to citizens' rights when dealing with law enforcement.

☐ 5 ☐ 4 ☐ 3 ☐ 2 ☐ 1

40. I have a clear understanding of how to speak to the police.

☐ 5 ☐ 4 ☐ 3 ☐ 2 ☐ 1

41. I know what to do if the police want to enter my home, but do not have a search warrant.

☐ 5 ☐ 4 ☐ 3 ☐ 2 ☐ 1

42. I know which Constitutional Amendments give me my rights against the police unreasonably searching and seizing my things or myself.

☐ 5 ☐ 4 ☐ 3 ☐ 2 ☐ 1

43. I have a clear understanding of what things to do to discourage the police from raiding any party that I throw.

☐ 5 ☐ 4 ☐ 3 ☐ 2 ☐ 1

44. I have a clear understanding of what to do if the police want to arrest me at my house.

☐ 5 ☐ 4 ☐ 3 ☐ 2 ☐ 1

45. I understand when and how to ask for an attorney if I am arrested.

☐ 5 ☐ 4 ☐ 3 ☐ 2 ☐ 1

46. I have a clear understanding of what behaviors and clothing styles bring on police attention.

☐ 5 ☐ 4 ☐ 3 ☐ 2 ☐ 1

47. I understand how to handle a situation in which the police want to search my car.

☐ 5 ☐ 4 ☐ 3 ☐ 2 ☐ 1

48. I understand what to do if I get pulled over by the police.

☐ 5 ☐ 4 ☐ 3 ☐ 2 ☐ 1

49. I can recognize when the police are supposed to read me my rights.

☐ 5 ☐ 4 ☐ 3 ☐ 2 ☐ 1

50. I know what rights I have if I am arrested.

☐ 5 ☐ 4 ☐ 3 ☐ 2 ☐ 1

Sample Search and Arrest Warrants

Court Case # 10987

STATE OF FORRESTOR, MUSTANG COUNTY

SEARCH WARRANT

TO: Any officer authorized by law to execute a search warrant in the County wherein the described property is located.

IN SAID COUNTY:

WHEREAS, on this day, Friday, April 12, 2051, Officer Peter Grimes of the Forrestor State Police has presented to me a sworn and signed affidavit stating facts sufficient to show probable cause for the issuance of a search warrant. Therefore, you are hereby commanded to:

A.   Search the person(s), premises, vehicle(s) described as follows:

922 Beachfront Way, Drenville, Mustang County, further described as a one-story ranch style home with burnt orange brick exterior, with a scarlet red carport attached and artificial grass covering the entire front yard.

A powder blue 2052 Mercedes Benz with royal blue interior and leather seats with Forrestor registration 1234567 and VIN# 1AEIO23U45Y6789.

B.   Seize the following property:

Crack cocaine and any items used in the consumption and manufacturing of crack cocaine, including but not limited to cocaine (whether in "rock" or powder form), sodium bicarbonate, and/or ammonium. Items to be used in the processing, use, storage, packaging, weighing, and distribution of crack cocaine.

Personal records and documents to aid in identifying a person or person(s) involved in the manufacturing activity. The records shall include but shall not be limited to records establishing ownership, dominion, or rental of the property(ies) named above in Section A. Computers, hard drives, recording devices of any kind, and images stored on any or all of these.

C.   Safely secure the seized property and make a return of this warrant to the undersigned judge within 5 days of its execution, with a written inventory of the property seized. To the person from whom the property is taken or from whose location or vehicle the property is taken, a copy of this warrant shall be given together with a receipt for such property. If said person is not present, a copy of this warrant and receipt may be posted at the place from where the property is taken.

D.   Execute this warrant within 10 days of this date. A return of Service for this Search Warrant, along with a listing of evidence seized thereunder, will be filed with the Clerk of the Court within (3) days from the date of service.

DATED on: _April 12_____, 2051, at Mustang County, Forrestor

Judge Willie D. Barrister

SEARCH WARRANT

STATE OF ROBOKEN, COUNTY OF ARVIN   DISTRICT COURT

TO: PEACE OFFICER(S) OF THE STATE OF ROBOKEN.

Affidavit having been made before me by Officer Bill Thomas has this day on oath, made application to the said Court applying for issuance of a search warrant to search the following described: Premises, Motor Vehicles(s), Person:

1250 Westerville, Lodi, Roboken 59146; a single-family two-story contemporary residence with orange siding and a one car garage. The home has a green front door and the numbers 87 are posted in silver to the left of the front door.

2020 Toyota Camry, RB license plate: WUB-099, VIN: 8R3RJ94795FK936612

Hailey Jane Thomas, DOB: 6/17/1990
Mark Alan Lohan, DOB: 1/23/1992
Rolondo Jermiah Ruffin DOB: 5/30/1996

There is now located certain instruments, articles, or things, namely:

- Assembled improvised incendiary devices and unassembled components of these devices, to include, fire bombs, glass containers such as bottles and jars; wicks such as cloth, paper and twine; enhancers such as Styrofoam and soap flakes.
- Ignitable liquids to include but not limited to gasoline, diesel fuel, kerosene, mineral spirits, lamp oil and brake fluid
- Assembled improvised explosive devices and unassembled components of these devices, to include but not limited to, metal glass, plastic and cardboard containers.
- Potential explosive materials and liquids such as chlorine derivatives, acids, fuels, and oxidizers.
- Manuals, books and/or instruction for the construction of improvised explosives.
- Explosive filler materials to include pyrotechnic powder; propellants such as black powder, smokeless powder, pydrodex and flash powder, match heads.
- Computer systems, including but not limited to, the main computer box, monitors, scanners, printers, modems and other peripheral devices.
- Media in whatever form, including, but not limited to, magnetic (such as floppy disks, hard drives and magnetic tape), flash (such as media cards and USB thumb drives) or optical such as compact disks and digital video disks).
- Digital camera equipment.
- Electronic devices, including but not limited to, MP3 players (including, but not limited to iPods) gaming systems, cellular phones and personal digital assistants (PDAs).
- Programs and manuals related to operating systems or applications.
- Proof of residency and documentation relating to the Internet, including but not limited to bills from Internet Service Providers (ISP).
- Proof of residency and related documents to show constructive possession of property.

- Data contained on either hard drives, electronic devices or removable media and all items being sought to include deleted files, archived files and email files.
- Data contained within any seized cellular phone, SIM card, PDA or electronic device to include, but not limited to, call logs, contacts, text messages, audio messages, images, Internet cache and deleted data.
- Information showing ownership, possession and use of the computer(s) and electronic device(s), including but not limited to e-mail accounts, screen names, and Internet accounts.

WHEREAS, the application and supporting affidavit of Commander Jameson was duly presented and read by the Court, and being fully advised in the premises.

NOW, THEREFORE, the Court finds that probable cause exists for the issuance of a search warrant upon the following grounds:

1. The possession of the property above described constitutes a crime.
2. The property above was used as a means of committing a crime.
3. The property above described constitutes evidence which tends to show a crime has been committed, or tends to show that a particular person has committed a crime.
4. The property above described is in possession of a person with intent to used such property as a means of committing a crime.

The Court finds that probable cause exists to believe that the above described property and things (are) (will be) at the above described premises, and on the person (s) of **see above**.

The Court finds that a nighttime search is necessary to prevent the loss, destruction, or removal of the objects of said search. Also to protect the officers and the public.

The Court further finds (does not find) that entry without announcement of authority or purpose is necessary (to prevent the loss, destruction, or removal of the objects of said search) (and) (to protect the safety of the peace officers).

 NOW, THEREFORE, YOU DEPUTY CHIEF MARC GRIMES, LODI POLICE DEPARTMENT OR THE PEACE OFFICERS(S) AFORESAID, AND ALL OTHER PERSONNEL UNDER YOUR DIRECTION AND CONTROL ARE HEREBY COMMANDED TO SEARCH THE DESCRIBED PREMISES, THE DESCRIBED MOTER VEHICLE(S), FOR THE ABOVE-DESCRIBED PROPERTY AND THINGS, AND TO SEIZE SAID PROPERTY AND THINGS AND TO RETAIN THEM IN CUSTODY SUBJECT TO COURT ORDER AND ACCORDING TO LAW.

BY THE COURT:

Robert Thomas

Date: July 13, 2022

JUDGE OF DISTRICT COURT

STATE OF ROBOKEN
COUNTY OF ARVIN

___DISTRICT_____ COURT, ARVIN COUNTY, ROBOKEN

Criminal Action Number _L0052021CR556921-4_____

WARRANT FOR ARREST UPON AFFIDAVIT

BEFORE THE HONORABLE ___Jane Ralston_____

The People of the State of Roboken,
To: Any person authorized by law to execute arrest warrants.

You are hereby commanded to arrest the person of: Billy Bob Ampersand

DOB:	**5-19-99**	HAIR:	BROWN
HEIGHT:	**6'1"**	EYES:	BROWN
WEIGHT:	**198**	RACE/SEX:	MALE
DL#:	**ROBOK L8358393**	SSN:	████████
ALIAS:	**HERBERT**	ALIAS D.O.B.	

And take the person above-named without necessary delay before the nearest judge of the Court of Record, to be advised that the person is being held for the alleged commission of the following crime(s), to-wit: In violation of OCC., 1980 revised:

Charge #	OCC #	Charge	Classification
1	17-2-105(a)	Murder (First Degree) – After Deliberation	F 1
2	17-2-105(b)	Murder (Second Degree) – Felony Murder	F 1

That this warrant for arrest is issued upon affidavit sworn to and affirmed before this court and relating facts sufficient to establish probable cause that the above-named offense has been committed and probable cause that the person named in this warrant committed that offense.

BAIL IS SET AT $ _Bond Denied_ WITH CONDITION(S)

DATE: _3/12/21_

_____
Judge's Signature

Agency Case Report # 79DA98624
Officer Name Cody B. Mitchell
Agency Arvin District Attorney's Office

RETURN OF SERVICE

I hereby certify that I have duly executed this warrant on this _____ day of _____ ,20___,

by _____ as I am herein commanded.

SHERIFF FEES:
Service $ _____
Mileage $ _____   By: _____
Return $ _____   Deputy
Total $ _____

Quick Order Form

For credit card orders, please visit our website at:
www.copscomeknockin.com

To order by mail, you may use this form. Please make your check or money order payable to: *Torinity, LLC.*

Name: _____

Address: _____

City: _____ State: _____ Zip:_____

Telephone: _____

Email address: _____

Item	Price	Quantity	Totals
When The Cops Come Knockin' School and Organization Edition	$29.99		
Sales Tax 7% (Georgia Residents)			
Shipping and handling in the U.S.: $4.00 for the first book and $2.00 for each additional book.			
S & H International: $9.00 for first book: $5.00 for each additional book.			
		Total	

Please send your order to: Torinity Publishing Company
3645 Marketplace Blvd.
Suite 130-333
East Point, GA 30344

Or Call 1-800-552-0762, ext. 500